*Praying for Your
Unbelieving
Husband*
༄

Praying for Your Unbelieving Husband

∞

Michael and Diane Fanstone

SERVANT PUBLICATIONS
ANN ARBOR, MICHIGAN

This edition issued by special arrangement with Monarch Publications, Broadway House, The Broadway, Crowborough, East Sussex, TN61HQ, England.

Vine Books is an imprint of Servant Publications especially designed to serve evangelical Christians.

Published by Servant Publications
P.O. Box 8617
Ann Arbor, Michigan 48107

Cover design: Brian Fowler, DesignTeam, Grand Rapids, MI

97 98 99 00 10 9 8 7 6 5 4 3 2 1

Printed in the United States of America
ISBN 1-56955-032-8

LIBRARY OF CONGRESS CATALOGING-IN-PUBLICATION DATA

Fanstone, Diane
Praying for your unbelieving husband / Diane and Michael Fanstone.
    p. cm.
ISBN 1-56955-032-8
1. Wives—Prayer-books and devotions—English. 2. Husbands—Religious life. 3. Christian women—prayer-books and devotions—English. 4. Non church-affiliated persons. I. Fanstone, Michael J. (Michael John) II. Title
BV4844.F36 1997
242'.6435—dc21
                                                97-23735
                                                CIP

Acknowledgments

WE ARE VERY GRATEFUL to those who have helped us by reading and assessing the early drafts of our material. Sylvia Austin, Jenny Miller, Marion Sherwood, and Marion Thompson have made numerous suggestions which have resulted in the final text being much clearer and easier to read. We are very grateful to them all. However, we accept full responsibility for anything insensitive or unhelpful.

Introduction
❦

MARRIAGE CAN AND SHOULD BE a pleasurable and fulfilling experience, but if you are in a relationship as a Christian with someone who does not share your faith, it can lead to serious tensions.

We want you to know that we have written this book because we understand something of these stresses because of our counseling experiences. We recognize how difficult and demanding life may be for you at home, at least some of the time. This is not surprising if you and your spouse have different perspectives on something that is central to your life.

We have compiled this book because we want you to be encouraged. We do not have any quick-fix solutions. Our hope is to point you each day toward the God who will walk with you through everything you encounter.

It would be wonderful if we could promise that if you did this and prayed that, your husband would turn to Jesus Christ and all your problems would be solved. While we have no hesitation in assuring you that God will invest his resources to help that happen, it will also take an open mind and a willingness to change on the part of your husband before that great day comes.

There are sufficient devotions in the following pages to provide you with a different reading and meditation for about four months. Our overall goal has been to point you to God, encourage you to trust him, and suggest some positive things you can do or pray which could help your husband come to Christ.

We suggest that you pray each day on the theme of that day's meditation. To help you get started we have included the first sentence or two. After this comes either a question, which we encourage you to answer, or a practical task you could undertake, in order to leave you with something relevant to think about or do during the day.

We recognize that everyone's circumstances are different, and that some material will be more relevant for your situation than others. However, our prayer is that God will meet you, speak to you, and help you in a variety of ways as you use these devotions. Please write and tell us, via our publisher, if your life changes as you read and use this book.

Diane and Michael Fanstone
Gravesend, England
April 1997

Will He, Won't He? 1

Let us run with perseverance. HEBREWS 12:1

Read: Hebrews 11:32–12:3

An uncomfortable silence hung over the dining room as the family began their Sunday meal. Barb and her husband, Jim, had hardly spoken two words since she had returned from church with their three children.

"You missed a great service, honey," Barb smiled, trying to break the ice.

"Pass the mashed potatoes," was all her husband replied.

Barb tried again. "Don't you want to hear about it?"

"No, I don't want to hear about it," Jim said firmly. "I'm glad you enjoyed it, and I enjoyed my time alone here too. I told you this morning, I'm really not interested in church. Subject closed."

Barb was stunned. She just couldn't imagine what had prompted Jim's dramatic change of attitude. Three months earlier he had willingly gone with her and the children to a potluck supper and family fun night at church. He had not only enjoyed himself, but had easily talked with a number of Barb's church friends—people he had never met before. Since that night, he'd actually attended church with his family a few Sunday mornings and had begun to express some interest in Christianity. Barb had thought her prayers for her husband were finally being answered. And now this. He simply changed his mind about the whole thing. What was she to do?

Does this story remind you of your situation, or of a friend you care about? Perhaps your husband has also changed his mind over issues you hold dear—his eternal salvation and faith. Maybe he just doesn't understand your deep concern for him in this regard. It is heartbreaking to watch someone you love show no interest in the things of God, or seemingly have no thought of his eternal destiny. And, as with Barb Miller, it is especially difficult to see your loved one show hopeful signs of growing interest, only to suddenly and without explanation change his mind and turn away again.

God knows what you are going through as you persevere in prayer for your unbelieving husband, or for someone else you love. And yet his Word tells you to be encouraged, to know that he hears your prayers and is quietly at work in your husband's life, even if you can't see it right now. No matter what happens at home, keep your eyes on Jesus. God honors persevering faith.

Suggested Prayer

Lord, I confess I struggle when my husband's response to you changes for no apparent reason. Please increase my faith so that I can trust you to keep working in his life whether I see any obvious signs of response or not.

A Practical Suggestion

In order to maintain some Christian contact, arrange a time when you and your husband can meet socially with a couple he already knows and likes from your church. Plan a fun evening—perhaps a cookout and badminton in the backyard. Use your imagination!

The Pain of Being Misunderstood 2

No wound was found on him, because he had trusted in his God.
DANIEL 6:23

Read: Daniel 6:1-23

Having your motives questioned and loyalty doubted is painful—as Daniel discovered. He was wholly dedicated to serving King Darius, but when confronted with a clear choice of loyalty to God or the king, Daniel knew he had to put God first. He continued praying regularly and openly to God, knowing he might be severely punished, even killed for his faith.

Issues of loyalty are as real for us today as they were for Daniel in ancient Babylon. Joan, a young woman who had been happily married for two years, faced a difficult test of loyalty in her own home. She and David were both public schoolteachers with a great love for children. Highly dedicated to their work, neither of them had ever thought much about God or had felt a need for any kind of religious faith. Teaching was their life, and they found it a fulfilling profession to share as a married couple. Joan, however, had unspoken questions about God—questions she had never felt comfortable discussing with David. He seemed so self-sufficient, so capable, without need of any kind of religious "crutch," as he called it, to get through life.

Joan decided not to tell David when she accepted an invitation to join with a small group of teachers who met together before school each day for Bible study and prayer. Here, in the midst of their warm acceptance and care, she discovered God's love for her. She became a Christian after just a few visits, but found that her husband turned uncharacteristically antagonistic as soon as she told him about it.

Joan was faced with a dilemma. She desired nothing more than to love and be loved by both God and her husband at the same time. But David took her newfound faith as a threat to their relationship, a sharp departure from the life they had planned together. In his mind, she was no longer the woman he married. Joan worried now that she would have to choose between God and her husband.

Your relationship to God may also be misunderstood as your family interprets your faith as a threat. They may think you have become a religious fanatic and care less about them than you used to. Of course, you know this is untrue, and that your love toward them and commitment to them is not threatened at all by your love for God and desire to serve him.

God took good care of Daniel, but he had to spend the night with some hungry lions whose mouths God miraculously kept tightly closed. When others misunderstand you, remember that God knows your heart and motives and will support you too—even in the face of opposition in your own home.

Suggested Prayer
Lord, I want to keep close to you, but please help me to know if I am unnecessarily antagonizing members of my family by being insensitive. Help me to be loyal to both you and them—even if they do not understand my motives.

A Practical Suggestion
If someone you live or work with seems to misunderstand your faith, think of some new and positive ways to relate to them. Express an interest in one of their favorite activities—a sport or hobby. Find a non-threatening topic of conversation.

The Protective Hand of God 3

The Lord was with Joseph and he prospered. GENESIS 39:2

Read: Genesis 37:12-28

Joseph felt incredibly alone when his brothers sold him to Midianite merchants, who then took him to Egypt and traded him once again. At a single stroke, he was ruthlessly separated from his entire family. We can only imagine the intense pain of his separation; he must have especially missed his doting father's love and attention (37:3). Yet, despite the hardships Joseph had to endure, God had not forgotten him. He completely understood how Joseph felt and stayed close to him, gradually putting in place his plans for Joseph's future.

Christian wives can also know the pain of emotional or even physical separation from their husbands, when their faith is resented or misunderstood. One woman has said, "My becoming a Christian has meant leading separate lives, with different values and differing sources of enjoyment." Another agreed, saying, "I feel lonely and isolated because my husband has no concept of a spiritual life."

When you experience such times of loneliness or isolation from your husband or family, remember the story of Joseph—how God worked behind the scenes to work out his plan in Joseph's life. God is doing the same for you. He has already mapped out his future direction for your life. His invitation to you today is to trust him.

Suggested Prayer
Heavenly Father, please reassure me today that you are with me now and always will be—whatever happens. You have a wonderful plan for my life. Even when the way seems darkest, I will trust you. Let me sense your fatherly support and encouragement.

A Practical Suggestion
To help your husband know how much you still love him, ask him what he would like to do the next time you have some time off together. Then go along with him and enjoy his choice—even if you detest fishing!

4 *Learning to Forgive*

Do not let the sun go down while you are still angry. EPHESIANS 4:26

Read: Ephesians 4:17-27

Jane never anticipated the effect her newfound faith would have on her husband, Rob. From the moment she first told him of her response to Christ's love, he became angry, and while he remained fairly easygoing on the surface, he often seemed irritable and tended to criticize her with very little provocation. Try as she might, she could never find out why he was behaving like this toward her, and so she felt powerless to help heal the gaping wound that was developing in their relationship.

Jane knew from the teaching in her church how crucial it is for Christians not to hold on to resentment and bitter feelings, or to let relationship problems fester by allowing unresolved tensions to remain unattended. Whenever she could, in any area of life, Jane faced problems head on so that she could sleep with a clear conscience. Ironically, it was a problem she faced at home that seemed impossible for her to get a grip on.

Coping with her ongoing difficulty was demanding and draining for Jane because, apart from other reactions, she felt guilty at her inability to put things right. There was nothing she could do about it, however, for Rob simply would not discuss it.

When Paul wrote to the Ephesian Christians, he told them how, as Christ's disciples, they were to "speak truthfully" (v. 25) and make genuine attempts to restore relationships whenever they could. God does not hold us accountable when those we love refuse to respond to our efforts to make things right. We are simply to do whatever we can to maintain healthy relationships and trust God to do the rest. If we keep this as our goal, we will undoubtedly know God's continuing help and support.

Suggested Prayer

Dear Lord, please help me to remain committed to restoring any relationship in my life that is strained, however long it takes. I want all the relationships in my life to please you.

A Question to Answer

Have you attempted to understand why there are difficulties in any of your relationships? Choose one that is troubling you and think through the whole situation in detail from the other person's perspective. Ask God for his unique insight. Write down any specific steps you feel God might be asking you to take in mending or strengthening that relationship.

5

A Gift to the Lord

So now I give him to the Lord. 1 SAMUEL 1:28

Read: 1 Samuel 1:21-28

It was Angie's thirteenth birthday—a milestone day in her young life as she embarked on her teen years. Noreen and Don wanted to make it a special morning for their daughter before she left for school, so they surprised her with her favorite breakfast and a present they felt certain she would not be expecting.

"Oh, you didn't!" Angie exclaimed as she tore the wrapping off of a CD player she had begged her parents to let her buy just last month. After telling her it was much too expensive, they decided to surprise her with it on this special birthday. Angie could hardly contain herself and gave her parents a big hug before running to catch the school bus.

Later, when everyone had left the house and Noreen had a moment alone before heading off to work, she smiled to herself at the delight on Angie's face when she saw the CD player. Noreen thanked God for her daughter and began to pray for her. She was startled to sense God's quiet voice in her heart, telling her that the very most important gift she could ever give her daughter was her prayers—specific prayers covering all aspects of her child's life and future. Noreen gained a new understanding that special morning: as a Christian wife and mother, her prayers for her family were the greatest gift she could ever give them.

The prophet Samuel's mother, Hannah, also understood the importance of a mother's prayers. When Samuel was born, Hannah had no doubt that God had intervened and answered her many prayers for a child of her own (1 Sm 1:11). Samuel was very young when she dedicated him to God's service. She did so, not only because she had made a binding promise, but because she had a deep confidence in God. If Samuel lived according to God's divine plan as he grew up, then his life would be fulfilling and would bring glory to God.

All parents are called by God to pray for their children. If our spouse is not a believer, that is all the more reason to pray faithfully ourselves. It is the most responsible thing any Christian parent can ever do, and also our greatest privilege.

Suggested Prayer

Heavenly Father, please help me to pray for my family each day, then having prayed, to follow Hannah's example and not snatch them back—as if their spiritual future is my responsibility. I give them to you and know that you will take very good care of them.

A Practical Suggestion

Make a prayer journal for each day as a reminder to pray regularly for your children. Remember their schooling, friendships, relationships, protection in teenage years, conversion to Christ, spiritual growth, their future partners, and maybe even their future children.

Belonging Together

Though all its parts are many, they form one body.
1 CORINTHIANS 12:12

Read: 1 Corinthians 12:1-14

Things were not right and Janice knew it. Going to church was getting more and more difficult because she only made it once in a while. Her husband, Terry—in order to avoid having to go to church himself—kept arranging for them to go out together on Sunday mornings to "enjoy the beauty of nature." Janice did enjoy their excursions—fishing or hiking in some of their beautiful county parks, either by themselves or with friends. But she really wanted to be in church on Sunday mornings. Her job as a legal assistant in a fast-growing law firm was stressful, especially since there were no other believers in her office. She was so tired every evening after work that she couldn't find the energy to attend one of her church's week-night Bible studies. Church on Sunday morning afforded her the only opportunity all week to be with Christian friends and be encouraged in her faith. The longer she stayed away, however, the harder it was to relate to her church friends when she did get there. She found herself increasingly uncomfortable when they asked, "Where were you last Sunday? We missed you." *Should I just stop going to church altogether?* she wondered. *Is it so wrong to be outside enjoying nature with my husband on Sunday mornings?*

When Paul wrote his first letter to the church at Corinth, he could not emphasize enough how much all Christians belong together and need each other (1 Cor 12). To him, mutual fellowship, along with sharing the spiritual gifts God has given every Christian, was not of secondary importance to our other relationships. On the contrary, he believed staunchly that Christianity which ignores the corporate element is hardly recognizable as Christianity at all. If, like Janice, your involvement at church is limited and your relationships shallow, try not to give up. Even if you can't be there every week, stay involved as much as you can. The reality is that you need those other Christians, and *they need you*!

Suggested Prayer

Lord, help me to grasp the importance you place on Christians relating closely together as your family on earth. If I am ever in danger of becoming isolated, please alert me, and show me how to stay in fellowship with other Christians.

A Practical Suggestion

List some times you can remember that another Christian has taught, encouraged, or helped you in any way. Then list some times that you have helped or encouraged another Christian. Thank God for those members of his family who have contributed to your Christian life, and those with whom you have enjoyed fellowship.

When Things Go Sour

They had such a sharp disagreement. ACTS 15:39

Read: Acts 15:36-41

Christians who are married to unbelievers must live with the constant tension of not being able to share the same values and goals with their mates. Although life may be peaceful at times, there is always the threat of conflict when certain subjects come up. Even the apostle Paul and his close friend and colleague Barnabas had a serious argument over whether or not they should take John Mark on a missionary trip. Because Mark had deserted them once before, Paul felt the young man was a liability, while Barnabas sensed he should be given a second chance. For some reason they were completely unable to resolve their disagreement, and they split up. If Christians can disagree so strongly at times, then surely we can understand why we will have difficulty living in complete peace with a non-believing partner.

After fifteen years of marriage, Margaret and Brad generally got along well, but the issue of Margaret's faith, and her desire to meet with other Christians, was virtually guaranteed to cause disruption to their household. She often compromised her own desires by missing meetings at church because she feared an argument at home if she said she was going. She grew accustomed to this situation after so long, but it made her sad.

Are situations like Margaret's hopeless? Should she anticipate having to cope with the same problems for the rest of her life? God can help us to reconcile our differences with those we love in any number of ways. He helped the apostle Paul see John Mark in a different light and they were reconciled. Second Corinthians 6:14-18 makes it clear that sharing a home with an unbeliever will be difficult and may lead to many conflicts. But if we ask in faith, believing in his promises to us, God can help us live in peace with others in our lives, even those who do not share our Christian faith.

Suggested Prayer

Please help me to trust you, Lord, when we experience conflict at home because I want to be faithful to you. Please support me, and help me to be particularly sensitive and conciliatory when I can.

A Practical Suggestion

Cook your husband one of his favorite dishes for dinner tonight.

Live a life of love. EPHESIANS 5:2

Read: Ephesians 4:29—5:7

Rachel had taken her three children to the park, and from a distance she stood watching them play—first on the swings, then on the slide, and finally on the merry-go-round. They never seemed to get tired, even though they stayed in the thick of the action most of the time. Shivers went down Rachel's spine as she saw them hanging on precariously while other children pushed the merry-go-round ever faster. Once, she even closed her eyes rather than see what would happen next!

As she reflected, Rachel realized she had a tendency to act at home like her children did in the park. Her husband, Ron, was not a practicing Christian, but because Rachel's personal faith meant so much to her, she never tired of finding ways to tell him how much he needed to believe in Jesus Christ, too. Watching the children at play, she now understood that her constant nagging could be pushing her husband precariously close to rejecting Christianity for good.

Paul's encouragement to the Ephesian Christians was to *live out* their faith, and he drew their attention to the example of Jesus, who "gave himself as a fragrant offering and sacrifice." Ultimately, it was what Jesus did that paid the price for mankind's sin, not what he said. Ron is more likely to respond to Rachel's faith if she concentrates on living it out rather than harassing him verbally. There is great power in the witness of a loving life.

Suggested Prayer
Lord, please help me get to know you better—in a personal and intimate way—so that I can imitate you more, especially at home.

A Question to Answer
Are there any particular things you tend to do or say regularly that create barriers between you and your husband, making it harder for him to relate to the gospel? Try to avoid them.

Having Mutual Respect

Bear with each other. COLOSSIANS 3:13

Read: Colossians 3:1-17

Valerie and John used to attend church together when they first married, but as the years went by, he found other things to do on Sundays and preferred to stay at home while she went alone. This led to increasing friction between them, for while John became less and less interested in spiritual issues, Valerie found that her faith was growing and God was becoming more important to her. Their problems only got worse whenever they tried to discuss issues of significance.

One day it dawned on Valerie how much she resented and even disliked John. The more she thought about it, the more she worried as to where her feelings could lead. Wisely, she decided to talk to a church counselor, who showed her that, as far as possible, she needed to understand, love, and respect her husband—despite their different priorities. The counselor reminded Valerie that one of the great strengths of Christianity is that, with God's help, Christians can display a tolerance and acceptance of those who irritate them. Jesus' love is such a powerful resource that we can even respond with dignity and respect—as Jesus did when he was opposed.

If there is one thing that eventually may bring John to Jesus Christ, it will be Valerie's respect and love for him—especially when he least deserves it. However, in the meantime, Valerie needs to be patient and faithful for as long as it takes.

Suggested Prayer
Although I sometimes find it hard to be tolerant, Lord, help me today to appreciate the good things about my husband, and to respect his views—even if I cannot agree with them. Help me to become more like Jesus.

A Question to Answer
If Jesus lived in your house, how do you think he would handle your husband's feelings about him and the church?

10   *The Annoying Drip*

A quarrelsome wife is like a constant dripping. PROVERBS 19:13

Read: Proverbs 19:1-14

The Book of Proverbs is full of God's wisdom on how to live. In today's verse, wives are reminded that relentless arguing or nagging tends to irritate like the constant dripping from a leaky kitchen faucet. However well-intentioned a Christian wife may be, she is more likely to see her husband show interest in her faith if she witnesses constantly by her life and only occasionally by her words, and if she prays regularly for God's revelation to break through to her husband's heart and mind.

Today's verse from Proverbs helped to save Julie's marriage. She was so excited about her faith that she just couldn't help urging Kevin every day to consider the claims of Christ. No one doubted Julie's motives, least of all Kevin, but he knew for certain that her faith was not for him. When she first told him she wanted to go to church, he found it amusing. He reacted with characteristic caution but did not stand in her way. However, once she became a Christian and wanted to spend more time with her church friends, he got a little irritated. Kevin really stopped seeing the funny side of it when Julie began to pressure him into going to church with her. He had made up his mind long before that religion was not for him, and Julie's daily pestering began to drive a wedge between them. Their marriage was falling apart at the seams.

Then one day as Julie spent some quiet time in prayer, God used this verse from Proverbs to open her eyes. She suddenly understood how much damage her attitude was causing in her marriage. With God's help she determined to back off and let him be the one to change Kevin's heart. Kevin is not yet a Christian, but he is seeing his wife in a new light, and his own attitude toward her faith has become more accepting.

Do you find it difficult—maybe impossible—to keep from nagging your husband about the Christian faith? God knows your heart ... he knows how much you love your husband and want him to be reconciled to Jesus Christ and come into his kingdom. Ask him to keep you from being the nagging wife that Proverbs describes. Instead of a constant dripping, be a source of refreshment and joy to the people you love.

Suggested Prayer

Father, please give me wisdom to control my enthusiasm for you, by being very careful what I do and say in front of close members of my family who do not yet know you. May my life shine for you and my prayers for them be answered.

A Practical Suggestion

Make a point of listening carefully to yourself during an hour spent with your husband. Then try to put yourself in his shoes and evaluate the way you behaved and the words you spoke. Try to assess whether you helped draw him closer to yourself as his wife, and to God's kingdom, or whether you pushed him further away.

God Is Fair with Everyone

There is no favoritism with him. EPHESIANS 6:9

Read: Ephesians 6:5-9

"I just don't understand," Jean said to Hazel in a puzzled voice. "I've been a Christian for almost eight years and I've done everything I know to get Roger to become a Christian, but he still isn't the least bit interested. He only comes to church at Christmas because I threaten to make a scene when his parents visit if he doesn't. Janet has only been a Christian for eighteen months, yet she told me yesterday that her husband responded to the altar call on Sunday and became a Christian. He only began coming to church a month ago. I really don't think it's fair. Why doesn't God answer *my* prayers?"

We can see why Jean feels upset, hurt, bewildered, and possibly angry. It looks as if God has overlooked her, while showing special favor to Janet. The psalmist felt the same way in Psalm 44:23-24. It is at times like this, though, that we need to look more deeply at the underlying issues.

Today's passage includes Paul's teaching to masters and slaves, two very different groups of people. Their lifestyles were a million miles apart, and yet Paul spoke of how God views all human beings as equals, master and slave alike. God does not favor Janet over Jean, nor one husband over the other. He wants both of them in his kingdom and will keep sending his Holy Spirit to reveal more spiritual truth to Roger so that in due course, when he is ready, he can make his own personal response to Jesus.

Suggested Prayer

Lord, please help me not to get resentful when other people's prayers seem to get answered sooner than mine. Rather, encourage me to keep praying with even more passion for those who have not yet responded to your love.

A Question to Answer

What answers to your prayers has God given you in the past? Make a list of several of those answers as a reminder that God listens and responds to your prayers too.

God's Reluctant Missionaries

Jonah was greatly displeased and became angry. JONAH 4:1

Read: Jonah 4:1-11

Within months of their wedding, Elaine started to wonder if she should ever have married Stuart. Having become a Christian at fifteen, she had seen some of her school friends commit their lives to Jesus too, so, when she met Stuart and they fell in love, she presumed the same would happen to him. All he needed was time. Yet as their relationship grew deeper, she knew Stuart was not coming any closer to God. What troubled Elaine the most was the way Stuart began to use offensive, even blasphemous, language once they were married. Because of his attitude, Elaine finally assumed he would never become a Christian, and she stopped trying to tell him about Jesus. She did her best to keep her church friends away from her home because she expected Stuart to embarrass her. Nor did she want him to come to church with her; it was easier to keep the two areas of her life separate. Elaine had become a reluctant missionary in her own home.

Jonah, too, was a reluctant missionary. He had no desire at all to see God work in the lives of the Ninevites. To be honest, he detested them and thought they deserved God's harshest judgment, not his most generous mercy. Even after witnessing an outpouring of God's mercy on the wicked city of Ninevah, Jonah remained angry at the way God had worked through him.

The transforming miracle that God worked in the lives of the people of Ninevah shows the enormity of his power and love. Because of your personal circumstances, you may be a reluctant missionary too, but God may surprise you if you remain obedient to him.

Suggested Prayer
Heavenly Father ... like Jonah, I find it very easy to look at my situation through human eyes alone. Please give me a clear understanding of what you could accomplish through my life, and then fill me with your Holy Spirit so that it can happen.

A Practical Suggestion
Head for your local Christian bookstore and find a biography to read. Choose one that tells how God worked significantly in and through someone who offered his or her life to him. Be encouraged by it!

Don't you care that my sister has left me to do the work? LUKE 10:40

Read: Luke 10:38-42

When he arrived home from work, Bruce always seemed to find Jill at the table poring over the Bible and a pile of study books, and it was a source of considerable aggravation to him. In reality, of course, it only happened once or twice a week, but on these occasions, after his busy and demanding day at work, he himself had to start cooking dinner for the family. Jill was now an at-home mom taking care of their two preschoolers, so she ought to have dinner ready when he got home, Bruce reasoned. That had been their agreement when she quit work to stay home with the children.

For him, this raised the whole question of Jill's priorities. She wasn't trying to be difficult—but she did tend to get carried away and not know when to stop. Bruce saw it as a sign that her faith was much more important to her than he was, and he resented it.

Like Bruce, Martha was unhappy over her sister Mary's faith. While Martha slaved over a hot stove fixing a meal for Jesus, Mary sat listening to him. Martha thought this was unfair, and she appealed to Jesus for support. She must have been surprised to hear him commend Mary instead. He did so because he knew that the spiritual food he offered was more important than the food Martha was worrying about.

Our task is also to get our priorities right—not an easy thing to do. Usually we have to balance our many responsibilities against each other but, in view of Jesus' words, we need to make sure we neither ignore him nor the food!

Suggested Prayer

I struggle so often, Lord, when trying to assess what ought to be my priorities at any given time. Please guide me so that I neither compromise my faith by giving you too little time and attention, nor neglect my husband by seemingly communicating to him that he does not matter much to me.

A Question to Answer
Think through carefully and in detail the impression you gave your husband yesterday. Did your actions, attitudes, and words tell him that he is, for you, the most important person in the world?

She sent word to the rulers of the Philistines. JUDGES 16:18

Read: Judges 16:1-21

Margaret really enjoyed attending a group in her church for women whose husbands did not yet believe in Jesus. The most valuable part was finding that others understood exactly how she felt. At home, life was not easy for her. Her husband had been passed over for several promotions at work, and he was angry and resentful. To make matters worse, he did not appreciate Margaret's faith and the time she spent at church. Consequently, when Margaret was safely surrounded by her friends, she talked very openly about Bill. Sometimes her friends squirmed uncomfortably as she described things that happened at home. Eventually, the pastor's wife took Margaret aside and kindly suggested that she be more discreet in how much she divulged to the group in the future.

Wherever the dividing line is between what is confidential within a relationship and what can be shared outside of it, Delilah was clearly on the wrong side. Her sole intention was to betray Samson once he divulged the secret of his strength. Sadly, when he could no longer withstand her nagging and told her the truth, she revealed his secret to the Philistines, who took immediate advantage of him. Despite his love for her, Delilah had no sense of loyalty to him.

Proverbs 2:6 tells us that "the Lord gives wisdom." How valuable this special gift is when we need the discretion to know when to speak and when to keep quiet.

Suggested Prayer
Recognizing, Lord, that I often feel torn between different people to whom I have a sense of responsibility, I ask for your wisdom that I might say the right things. Please save me from making a habit of saying the wrong thing in the wrong place at the wrong time—but forgive me when I do.

A Practical Suggestion

If, like Margaret, you are in a position where you can easily slip into divulging what should be confidential between you and your husband, work out carefully now how much you feel comfortable telling your friends at church during the course of conversation. Then do not overstep the mark.

He Listens

15

The Lord remembered her. 1 SAMUEL 1:19

Read: 1 Samuel 1:1-20

Hannah's experience is a source of great encouragement to any praying woman carrying a heavy burden. God hears all our prayers but, for reasons best known to him, he keeps some of us waiting a long time for a definitive reply. We would much rather get a quick answer from God, but sometimes his "wait" signal means that he wants to teach us patience and perseverance as we continue to pray. Eventually Hannah's prayer was answered and she gave birth to a son, Samuel. But she had to wait a very long time.

Carol was another woman who knew the pain of unanswered prayer. She clearly identified with the pastor's sermon one Sunday morning when he spoke of the need for Christians to pray relentlessly. She and some of her friends had been praying for a very long time for her husband, Frank, to become a Christian, but so far the most encouraging thing to have happened was that one Christmas Eve he had gone to church for a candlelight service. Even that was three years ago, and there were times when Carol seriously considered stopping her prayers for him. She found the continual disappointment hard to cope with.

One day Carol thought about Hannah, and her faithfulness after years of unanswered prayer. The story of this courageous woman of the Bible spoke to Carol's heart and eased her burden. She knows that this by no means guarantees her the answer she longs for, but the mere fact that God still listens after years and years of praying the same prayer is a source of great encouragement to her.

Suggested Prayer

Heavenly Father, I am aware that, being human, I want what I pray for right away. Despite my impatience, help me to keep praying so that my faith in you grows through this experience of waiting. Then, Lord, when you do start to speak to my husband, please help him to be ready to respond to you.

A Practical Suggestion
Let God know how serious you are. Why not tell him that your husband's conversion is so important to you, you promise to pray every day until your husband comes to faith?

It's Hard to Believe

16

Sarah laughed to herself. GENESIS 18:12

Read: Genesis 18:1-15

Abraham's wife Sarah had thought it bizarre when she heard the prediction that she would bear a child at the age of ninety. She perceived it to be totally impossible, but she hadn't taken into account the kind of miracles God can do.

Neither had Liz, a young woman who had been married for five years to a man she deeply loved, but who she was certain would never become a Christian. One evening at a home Bible study group she attended, she found herself struggling with the message. They were discussing possible miracles, when her friend Virginia asked her pointedly, "Wouldn't it be fantastic if Greg became a Christian this year?"

Inside, Liz laughed. She knew it could not happen. She lived with Greg, and she knew him only too well. When she married, she had done so against the advice of her friends at church, who knew Greg was not a committed Christian. Her goal had been to see him converted, but instead, as the years had gone by, he had slipped farther away from God, and now she despaired of Greg's ever coming to God. Virginia's question was painful because it was well beyond what Liz could believe in at present.

What Liz had not realized yet is that God's power is unlimited. True, before anyone can become a Christian, that person needs to be open to hearing from God. But who knows what God may do next?

Suggested Prayer
Thank you, Lord, that despite Sarah's inability to believe, you gave her a son at the age of ninety. Please work out your plans for my family and me, even if my faith to believe in miracles is smaller than I would like.

A Practical Suggestion
Make a list of ten or twenty things God has done for people you know. Then thank him for his miracles.

17

A New Creation

If anyone is in Christ, he is a new creation. 2 CORINTHIANS 5:17

Read: Galatians 5:13-26

Claire had been a Christian for six months. She had become a Christian through the quiet witness of her best friend, Sue. While having coffee together one morning, Claire asked how she could be the same quiet witness to her husband, Joe, that Sue had been to her. Claire explained that it was not so much what Sue had talked about, but the life she lived that had made an impact on her. Sue suggested that Claire read Galatians 5:22, which talks about the fruit of the Spirit: love, joy, peace, patience, kindness, goodness, faithfulness, gentleness, and self-control.

As she read, Claire could also see what the Bible reveals in the pre-ceding verses (5:19-21), about the sort of life lived by many who do not yet believe. She realized afresh that once someone becomes a Christian, God begins to work deeply in that life. At this point a new person begins to emerge.

Claire needs to develop her relationship with Jesus by spending time getting to know him better. We do too. Then gradually, but definitely, the fruit of the Spirit will begin to become part of our lives and people will see that we are different. That in itself will be a witness to the Lord, and could well be the means by which other people, and especially those with whom we live, will see the reality and relevance of the Christian faith.

Suggested Prayer

Lord, thank you for all those Christians whose quiet witness has inspired and encouraged me. Help me develop my relationship with you so that others will see you in me.

A Question to Answer

Will you promise God that you will spend some time quietly each day, seeking to deepen your relationship with him, so that his fruit may begin to become part of your life?

The Lord is with you when you are with him. 2 CHRONICLES 15:2

Read: 2 Chronicles 14:2—15:4

When she was single, Georgina did not realize the importance of the Christian fellowship and spiritual teaching she received in her church's youth group. Now, though, Georgina was in her early thirties, married with two young children. With her marital and parental responsibilities and part-time job, she had plenty to do. She was aware she had had no contact with Christians since she moved to her new home, but thought she could manage spiritually as things were, maybe getting back into a church when the children were older.

The last thing Georgina expected in her life was tragedy, but a phone call one morning brought news that her father had suddenly died of a heart attack. Her life crumbled and she felt desperately lonely and sad, as one of the secure foundations in her life had been ripped from under her.

Thoughts of God flooded her mind. She recalled her previously close relationship with him and remembered how, whenever she drew close to him, he had come close to her. As Georgina cried to God, repented for ignoring him for so long, and turned back to him, he started becoming more real to her again. The same thing happened as in the days of Asa when God responded so warmly to the sincere cries for help from his people. Georgina's grieving was still long and painful, but she knew God was supporting her. Even her husband was surprised at how well she coped. Now God could begin to reach out to him....

Suggested Prayer
Father ... as I cry to you for help today, recognizing how far I have strayed from you, please receive me back.

A Question to Answer
Compared to the closest you have ever sensed you were to God, where are you today?

19 *Living in Christ*

Just as you received Christ Jesus as Lord, continue to live in him.
COLOSSIANS 2:6

Read: Colossians 2:6-15

Jason did not think he was disparaging about Ruth's faith, but ever since they had married nine months earlier, she felt he spoke disapprovingly about her church involvement. She knew he did not understand it; that was obvious from the talks they had had with John, her minister, before their wedding. The pastor had picked up on Jason's cynicism about Christianity and had gently warned Ruth about it, but up until their wedding she had detected nothing. Now, just months later, she knew John had been right; Jason did have some kind of resentment about Christianity and gradually seemed to be releasing it into their marriage. Ruth was seriously worried, but was delighted one Sunday at church when John preached from Paul's letter to the Colossians.

His message was to all Christians: even though we've opened our lives to receive Jesus Christ as Savior and Lord, we will sometimes be tempted, when the difficult and demanding times come along, to jettison our commitment to Christ. John continued by saying that to do so would be to deny the wonderful work of love and grace God has already accomplished. Indeed, it is when times are hard that God can work deeply in Christians' lives, and rooting and strengthening takes place.

Having been on the verge of giving up, Ruth went home more determined than ever to stay close to God, and to encourage Jason to talk about his resentment. Only then, with God's help, could they deal with it together.

Suggested Prayer
Thank you, Lord, that you understand me when I feel I just can't take any more. Thank you, too, for your renewed strength and vision to carry on when I need it most.

A Question to Answer

Can you imagine how God would feel if you decided to stop loving and serving him? Try to think it through from his viewpoint and write down the emotions God might experience if you rejected him.

I will pay back four times the amount. LUKE 19:8

Read: Luke 19:1-10

When Beth met her friend Katie one morning at the supermarket, she knew something good had happened. Katie's face was radiant. Beth learned that Katie's husband, Jeremy, had committed his life to Jesus Christ the night before, and Katie was sure it meant an end to all their recent problems. A few weeks later, however, Beth saw Katie again and noticed that the glow was fading, and she was sounding worried. They discussed the situation and Beth discovered that Katie was disappointed and in danger of becoming disillusioned. She had expected all the disagreements at home to end once Jeremy became a Christian, but, on recent occasions, they had been as bad as ever. Beth wisely encouraged Katie to be patient and to realize that growth takes time.

The transformation of Zaccheus, who had a life-changing encounter with Jesus, shows us why Christian growth takes time. Not only did he have to repent of his past sin and put his trust in Jesus for the first time, but also, with God's help, he had to change his entire way of life. Zaccheus began at once. No longer was he going to be a money-hungry thief; he would be fair, just, and responsible. To show how different he would be, he made amends for all that he had dishonestly gained in the past. His new life in Christ began to show through quickly, but we can imagine that it would be quite a while before every aspect of his life was different. It would have taken some time for others, even those close to him, to get to know the "new Zaccheus," to believe he had really changed. And it would have taken some time for him to overcome long-practiced habits of deceit and manipulation.

For most new Christians, the process of changing their lifestyle to become more like Jesus takes a long time. It gradually goes on from the moment of conversion until death. The best thing for Katie is not to expect too much too soon. The great news is that for Jeremy, the process has begun!

Suggested Prayer

Please help me to be patient, Lord, whenever I meet a new Christian. Help me to recall how definitely, yet sometimes slowly, the life-changing power of Jesus has affected my own life.

A Practical Suggestion

Pick just one of the qualities of Jesus you know that you lack in your life, then pray for it and ask God to help develop it in you—starting today.

21

What God Knows

After their children had grown and left home, Pat and Carl realized a lifelong dream—to own their own business together. Carl had supported his family as a carpenter for many years, and Pat had successfully managed a number of home businesses as her children got older. With their parenting responsibilities behind them, they felt that together they could succeed at a full-time business, so they invested their life savings into a local hardware store. Their investment paid off, and Pat and Carl enjoyed the fruits of their successful business venture.

Even though they enjoyed their shared success in business, on a personal level Pat felt their marriage was terribly lacking. Her husband knew very little about God and never showed any interest in discovering what Pat had experienced of God's love and care in the many years she had been a Christian. As a couple, they could talk easily about profit margins and ad campaigns, or where to go on their next vacation, but Carl would never discuss spiritual issues. He would never have acknowledged God's hand in their successes in life, preferring instead to think it was all their own doing.

To others in their community, Pat and Carl seemed to have a good marriage, but Pat knew their relationship remained on a very superficial level. She had lived and worked with this man for over thirty years, but his spiritual life and deeper longings were a complete mystery to her. Pat really wanted to know how he felt about God.

Then one evening in her Bible reading she discovered Psalm 139. God spoke clearly to her through it, and reminded her that not only does he know everything about her, but he is also fully aware of every aspect of Carl's life too. God made Carl and he knew him before he was born. He knows every choice Carl makes. He knows his thoughts and is even aware of the words that will come out of Carl's mouth before anyone hears them.

These truths are now real to Pat, and she no longer worries about Carl. Even if Carl seems to have no interest in God, God is clearly interested in him. Because of this, Pat can pray more confidently that Carl will eventually come to God through faith in Jesus. God has intimate knowledge of the life of every human being on earth ... and that includes you and your husband too.

Suggested Prayer

Lord, please help me to pray for my husband with the knowledge that you know all about him, and love him even more than I do.

A Practical Suggestion

Read through these verses slowly and meditate on them again. Consider carefully how your life might change if you truly believed in God's intimate knowledge of you and everyone you love.

22 *Doing It God's Way*

Let all the other men go. JUDGES 7:7

Read: Judges 7:1-22

Judy was quite skilled at practical jobs around the home. When a closet needed extra shelves, when the kitchen sink stopped up, or when the lawn mower broke down, Judy, armed with her toolbox, came to the rescue. Toby, her husband, gladly let her handle most of the household repairs, even though he was quite a handyman himself. It was just that Judy had a capacity to work out what was causing a problem, calculate the best way to fix it, and then set about to get the job done. Only rarely did she not succeed.

She used this same gift in the rest of her life too. She was especially helpful when friends had marriage problems, and when it came to how her own husband would become a Christian, Judy had it all worked out. She assessed how much exposure he would need to the gospel and how many contacts he would need with committed Christians. She even decided that in another few months, at the revival meetings her church was planning, Toby would walk to the front and dedicate his life to Jesus Christ.

In reality, Judy's plans were as humanistic as Gideon's. God needed to teach Gideon a vital lesson the night the Israelites defeated the Midianites. Gideon had to learn that divine plans are often a million miles removed from the best human solutions. What is more, they work much better. Judy needed to learn this too—and quickly, before she concluded that God had let her down. Her best course of action was to stop trying so hard to fix everything in life herself ... and to wait quietly for God to show her the *best* way.

Suggested Prayer

Please forgive me, Lord, when I try to do your job for you—and make things harder for you as a result. It is so good to know you have things under control.

A Question to Answer

Can you think of an occasion in the past when you came to your own conclusions as to how God would work, only to be taken aback when he did things differently? Repent if you need to, but take time to rejoice that God is so good.

Viewing Things God's Way

No longer two, but one.   MATTHEW 19:6

Read: Matthew 19:1-12

Diane was at the end of her tether. Life at home was virtually intolerable. While she believed that her husband, Jim, was the main problem because he worked all hours, she also knew that she had become increasingly intolerant and critical. Now that the children were on the verge of leaving home, she could not see how their marriage could survive. She consulted a lawyer for advice as she prepared herself for the divorce she believed inevitable.

The following Sunday Diane was at church, again without Jim, when the preacher highlighted the biblical teaching on marriage and divorce. To begin with, Diane found his insights helpful and illuminating, but she began to feel increasingly uncomfortable as she heard him stress the permanence of marriage (Gn 2:24). These are words that Jesus endorsed, adding that divorce was allowable in God's eyes only when one partner is sexually unfaithful. Diane knew that this was not the problem she faced, so she made an appointment to see her minister to discuss the situation.

Their conclusion, as they reflected on her circumstances, was that neither the spiritual incompatibility nor the deterioration in their relationship were grounds enough to consider divorce. God had recognized their union at the time of their marriage, and Diane's minister took time to encourage her to catch a fresh vision of what God could make of her marriage, and to pray constantly that Jim would become a Christian. He said, however, that the final decision as to whether or not she sought the divorce had to be hers....

Suggested Prayer
Please help me, Lord, to be able to see my situation at home clearly, and with insight that comes from you. Save me, I pray, from making any decisions, one way or the other, that later I will regret.

A Practical Suggestion
Find something positive and constructive you can do today to help improve your situation at home—even if it is small.

We did this ... to make ourselves a model for you to follow.
2 THESSALONIANS 3:9

Read: 2 Thessalonians 3:6-10

Cathy was becoming increasingly disillusioned by Rob's complete lack of interest in the Christian faith that was so important to her. In fact, she was so frustrated that one day, in her women's prayer group, she expressed herself quite angrily. "If my Christian life is so pathetic that Rob can't see how I've changed since I've become a Christian, is it worth going on?"

After the meeting the group leader, Anita, took Cathy aside. "Please don't do that again," she said. "If you feel uptight, come talk to me privately. Do you realize the effect your words might have had on Lindsay?"

To be honest, Cathy had not given Lindsay a moment's thought. Lindsay had only been a Christian for a few weeks, and she was absolutely sure that God's first task for her was to witness to her unbelieving husband. As Cathy thought about what Anita was telling her, she realized her angry words could have seriously discouraged Lindsay. "Please remember," Anita continued, "that as the older Christian, you have a responsibility to be a role model for those who have come to faith more recently."

Cathy had never considered this before, but it made sense to her. Paul taught the same vital truth. He knew how helpful it is when Christians who struggle to follow Jesus and become more like him have human examples to emulate. We all need role models to follow, as well as being role models for others. That places a great responsibility on *us* as well as Cathy.

Suggested Prayer
Father, please help me to follow Jesus faithfully, and then to realize that he wants to use even me as a role model for others. Help me, please, to be an encouragement to others.

A Practical Suggestion
List several ways in which another Christian you know has modeled Jesus Christ to you since you became a believer.

If two of you on earth agree about anything you ask for, it will be done.
MATTHEW 18:19

Read: Matthew 18:15-20

One day Hayley felt that God was leading her to pray harder for her family. She thought of her husband, George, whom she loved dearly, but who had not yet come to Christ, together with her two children, Alice and Paul, who were growing up fast. She wanted so much for her family unit to be solidly Christian, and found it hard to cope with things as they were.

On a camping vacation in the Rockies, as the children threw stones into the still water of a mountain lake, she noticed how, after the initial splash, circle after circle of ripples spread out over the surface. Hayley thought of the impact that prayer makes when God answers the heartfelt requests of his children, and especially of the way that God works when Christians pool their prayers and pray together. That day, as never before, she understood how both the Bible and so many Christian books are full of stories of the faithful way that God responds to his children's sincere prayers.

Jesus taught that prayer is powerful and effective, especially when two or more of his disciples join forces to pray. Paul reassures us in 1 Timothy 2:4 that God wants everyone to come to know him. Therefore, when we pray for our friends and families to find Jesus Christ as their Savior, we are praying in line with God's will. Who knows what will happen next as Hayley commits herself to pray more intensively than ever before?

Suggested Prayer
Please show me, Lord, how you want me to pray and with whom. I ask you to respond to my plea that my whole family will come to love and trust you too.

A Practical Suggestion
Find a group of three or four others who will join you in praying regularly for their families and yours to come to faith in Jesus Christ.

Going On Ahead

I am going ... to prepare a place for you. JOHN 14:2

Read: John 14:1-6

A pained expression was visible on Janna's face one morning as she knocked on her friend Maureen's door. "Can I talk with you?" Janna asked. "I'm worried about Jeff."

Maureen quickly invited her friend in and put on a pot of coffee. As they sat down together to talk, Janna explained. After her husband had gone to work that morning, and the children were off to school, she had opened her Bible to one of her favorite chapters: John 14. But instead of receiving comfort, her Bible reading caused her some concern. In one sense this was surprising, because Jesus was speaking of the preparations he is making for all his family to join him in heaven. This part of Jesus' teaching is virtually guaranteed to excite Christians ... but not Janna.

By no means was she feeling ungrateful to Jesus for what he had done and would do for her, but Janna's pain concerned Jeff, her husband. He expressed mild interest in her faith, but only sufficient to ask the occasional question and go to church with her once in a while. She loved him dearly, and desperately wanted him to believe in Jesus too, but so far he had made no decision to do so.

"What would happen if he had an accident and died suddenly?" she asked Maureen. "Would he go to hell?"

Maureen had considerable difficulty in giving Janna the reassurance she needed that day. Janna knew what the Bible had to say and believed it fully, and Maureen had to confirm that only those who personally trust Jesus will join him in heaven. Once Maureen had prayed for her, Janna was more aware again of her own salvation, but she left her friend's home more committed than ever to praying for Jeff.

Suggested Prayer

Lord, I am grateful for the promise to me of life in heaven with you. I pray again for my husband. Please reveal yourself to him so that we can look forward to heaven together.

A Practical Suggestion

Take some time to meditate on Jesus' words of reassurance about heaven. Think about what heaven will be like, and then pray that your husband will ask you a question one day soon that will allow you to share your thoughts with him.

Anyone who looks at a woman lustfully has already committed adultery with her in his heart. MATTHEW 5:28

Read: 2 Samuel 11:1-27

Jenny could hardly contain her excitement. "Oh," she gasped to Jeanette, who was sitting next to her in church. "Garth's preaching today, I'm so pleased." Garth was the youth leader in Jenny's church and preached only rarely. She found him extremely handsome with his boyish face, blond hair, and suntan. He also had an impish sense of humor, was a lively and effective communicator, and was obviously very close to God. In many ways he was everything that appealed to Jenny and was the virtual opposite of Gary, her husband, who resolutely refused to come to church, and sat at home glued to the sports channel on TV when he was not at work.

Things had gone further in Jenny's mind, however, than merely appreciating Garth as a preacher. She allowed her mind to wander sometimes and wondered how he performed in bed. She considered it harmless to speculate. After all, life with Gary was boring, tedious, and sometimes tense. Why was it so wrong to get a little mental pleasure? The fact that Garth was married was irrelevant; his pretty young wife was not affected by her private thoughts. She gazed lustfully at Garth as he began to preach, hardly hearing a word he said.

David's fling with Bathsheba was one of his biggest mistakes (v. 27). His adultery would never have taken place had he controlled his thoughts earlier on. Even though the Lord forgave him when he repented (see Ps 51), God was sad at this serious indiscretion. Jenny needs to be very careful.

Suggested Prayer

Please help me, Lord, to control my thoughts and not to be deceived by Satan into thinking that adulterous thoughts are acceptable. Rather, show me how to pray positively for my husband.

A Question to Answer

When you find yourself thinking or acting in a particular way, do you ask, "Would Jesus behave like this?"

The Difference That Counts

What does a believer have in common with an unbeliever?
2 CORINTHIANS 6:15

Read: 2 Corinthians 6:14-18

Megan had been far from happy when the minister of her church refused to marry her and Jonathan because she was a committed Christian and Jonathan was not. She felt it was unfair, but her minister saw their prospective marriage as contrary to the teaching of Scripture. He felt it was unwise for them to proceed, and impossible for the church to endorse the wedding and subsequent marriage. Eventually they decided to get married at another church where the minister wasn't so particular, but she felt let down. Megan, meanwhile, was determined to prove that she could still grow spiritually and be on fire for God, although married to an unbeliever.

For the first few years she seemed to be doing well, but as their tenth wedding anniversary drew near, the strain was beginning to tell. Jonathan had had phases when he seemed more responsive to Christianity, but they did not last. As Megan read the Bible, in between her less-frequent visits to church, she realized increasingly the truth of Paul's words describing the incompatibility of believers and unbelievers. It was true. She and Jonathan had different priorities and goals—not only different moral standards, but also completely different social interests and hobbies. It dawned on her that while she and Jonathan were moderately happy on the surface, they shared little at a deeper level.

This insight helped her to come to two conclusions. First, she realized that her church was not as unwise as she had originally thought. Second, she knew she needed to pray all the more for Jonathan to get to know Jesus personally.

Suggested Prayer

Lord, help me to face the reality of any past mistakes I have made. Forgive me as I confess, and strengthen me to keep growing in you.

A Practical Suggestion

While you and your husband may have deep differences that concern you, look for some activity you can enjoy together in the next day or two.

You would not listen to me. JEREMIAH 38:15

Read: Jeremiah 38:1-13

Fiona was doing her very best to convince her husband, Gerry, how important her faith was. She told him about Jesus' life, death, and resurrection, and the difference that his forgiveness, peace, security, and guidance made in her life each day. Even as she was speaking, she knew that Gerry was not really listening. His mind was clearly on other things, probably on the work that would occupy him the next morning. Fiona felt she had wasted her breath. Gerry had been polite, but seemed to ignore completely the best news he would ever hear. If only he would really listen....

Jeremiah, God's prophet, had to contend with exactly the same frustration. All he ever sought to do was to relay faithfully God's word to God's people, yet they were persistently unresponsive. What Jeremiah could not grasp was why they could see their plight but not recognize that trusting God was their only hope. His frustration reached an all-time high when he was imprisoned and later lowered into a well to die. His only crime had been to speak out God's word and truth.

Fiona, and others like her, have to recognize that those who need to hear God's word most may be among those who seem least inclined to receive it. However, God asks his people to faithfully declare it anyway. The ultimate responsibility for acting on it has to lie with the hearers. How sad for both Jeremiah and Fiona that their faithful words were not heeded....

Suggested Prayer
Please help me to be patient, Lord, when my words for you do not seem to elicit a response, but help me most of all to be faithful.

A Question to Answer
If your husband really will not listen when you tell him about Jesus, are you sure it is not because you preach at him, tell him in the wrong way—too often, or at the wrong time?

Each one heard them speaking in his or her own language. ACTS 2:6

Read: Acts 2:1-16

Lisa wanted God's special help. She longed for her husband, Bryan, to become a Christian, but she found that whenever she tried to talk with him about anything spiritual, it was completely the wrong time. He was never antagonistic, but sometimes he was preoccupied with work or was tired. Occasionally, though, he entered into lengthy discussions with Lisa about the reasons why he found coping with faith difficult. She always felt let down when a discussion ended before it had hardly begun. Her prayer was that God would give her a special gift of knowing when it was the best time to talk with Bryan.

On the Day of Pentecost the disciples of Jesus were given just such a gift. True, God's Spirit gave them the capacity to speak a variety of languages they had never learned, but the effect was that people who had not heard the Good News of Jesus discovered all about him as the Holy Spirit equipped the disciples to communicate simply but powerfully. As the Holy Spirit worked behind the scenes that day, three thousand people committed their lives to Jesus.

Lisa believed that if God had done it once, he could do it again. Why should he not guide her as to when to speak and when to keep quiet? Why should the Holy Spirit, who knows what Bryan is thinking, not guide her as to what subject to raise for discussion? For the sake of Bryan's conversion and God's glory, Lisa asked God for a special gift for her situation.

Suggested Prayer
Give me, I pray, a special gift of your Holy Spirit, Lord, so that I too may have that instinctive sense of what to say about you, when to speak, and when to be quiet. Please bring my husband to faith in Jesus soon.

A Question to Answer
Are you ready to be God's specific and sensitive mouthpiece at home? Tell God if you are.

Don't be afraid; just believe. MARK 5:36

Read: Mark 5:21-24; 35-43

Heather had a puzzled look on her face as she listened to her minister preach. He was explaining the extraordinary spiritual truth that, although anything God does is due ultimately to his remarkable and awe-inspiring power, he often involves people by working in partnership with them. Of course God can work independently, but so often he chooses to share what he does with people, in response to their simple trust and faith. It dawned on Heather that God might be offering her such an opportunity in order to see Bill, her husband, become a Christian. Until now, he had staunchly declined to bite on the carefully chosen and occasional words of witness she had expressed to him. Now, listening to the sermon, Heather's faith began to grow. If she simply trusted God for Bill to become a Christian and sought, with God's help, to live as a Christian at home, then maybe in due course Bill would respond to Jesus.

The four Gospels show clearly how much emphasis Jesus placed on the faith of individuals being the trigger that allows God's divine power to be released. Jairus had no doubt that Jesus could heal his daughter, and Jesus responded to this. Jesus' words, however, show that he was looking for faith in Jairus and his wife before the miracle would happen.

God still looks for simple trust in wives like Heather, whom he calls to work as his partners, so that, in his way and according to his time scale, he can do more miracles in people's lives.

Suggested Prayer
Heavenly Father, I recognize that faith is a spiritual gift. Please give me more.

A Question to Answer
Can you believe that Jesus could draw your husband into a personal relationship with himself? If you struggle to answer, ask God for more faith.

32   *The Pain of Separation*

If the unbeliever leaves, let him do so. 1 CORINTHIANS 7:15

Read: 1 Corinthians 7:1-16

Rosemarie's eyes were red as she picked up the phone and called her minister, Keith. During a fight the night before, her husband, Allen, had walked out of the house saying that if she insisted on believing this "garbage" about a first-century Jew called Jesus, she would have to live alone. With that he left, and now, the next morning, she had no idea where he was. Rosemarie had spent half the night sobbing into her pillow before falling asleep, exhausted. Now she needed her minister's support.

Keith first sought to establish how much Rosemarie's faith was really to blame in their relationship. Had she preached at Allen insensitively? No. Had she always insisted on going to church every Sunday irrespective of his wishes? No. Had she demanded that he go to church with her or believe what she did? No. As Keith listened, he heard a sad story which showed that an essentially happy marriage had changed from the day Rosemarie had first heard the gospel of Jesus. She had never expected to love Jesus in place of Allen; she saw from the beginning how different the two relationships were. Her long-term prayer was that Allen would want to love Jesus too so that they could be truly united spiritually.

Keith had to point Rosemarie to 1 Corinthians 7, though they prayed together that Allen would take time to reflect carefully on his marriage and what he stood to lose. What is more, Rosemarie dared to pray that Allen would work through his bigotry against Christianity and come to Christ, whether he returned to her or not. That is a brave prayer to pray!

Suggested Prayer

Lord, please minister very personally to me or any Christian wife who is in this sad situation. Give me your grace to respond in a way that will help my husband see your love in me.

A Question to Answer

If you and your husband disagree about your faith, are you sure that is really the problem in your relationship—or is it just a symptom?

Guard my life, for I am devoted to you. PSALM 86:2

Read: Psalm 86:1-13

Emily's patience was running thin because nothing seemed to be improving. She was fed up with the verbal abuse she had to tolerate at home from her husband. He had been in a state of rebellion and anger ever since she had first gone to an event at her local church, and that was three years before her conversion. For a reason she still did not fully understand, Stan had an aversion to religion, and Emily bore the brunt of his cynicism and temper. From the beginning she had struggled over how to cope with this, but because she did not want to speak ill of Stan in front of her church friends, she kept quiet and suffered in silence.

Even so, she was not inactive. When she had free time at home she found that she could pour out her hurt, anger, and frustration to God in the same way as the writer of Psalm 86 did centuries before. Both of them discovered the true sense of release there is in off-loading to God the problems they faced. The fact that she could be totally honest with God, without being disloyal to Stan, was also liberating, but Emily wanted a solution. While God's presence and strength were resources she could not do without, she desperately wanted the situation at home to change.

In this she was like the psalmist who wanted an "answer" (v. 1) and salvation from his dilemma (v. 2). He had no doubt that God could and would heed his passionate prayer (vv. 8, 10), and Emily also found that her faith in God grew as she kept praying for a remedy.

Suggested Prayer
Work in my life by your Spirit, I pray, Lord, so that as I trust you, you can answer my deepest needs and glorify yourself.

A Practical Suggestion
The writer of Psalm 86 was prepared to reaffirm his strong and loyal commitment to God *despite* his personal pain. Try this even if you do not feel like it. God will honor your commitment.

A Persuasive Argument

Do you think ... you can persuade me to be a Christian? ACTS 26:28

Read: Acts 26:1-32

Veronica was particularly interested in one session of a course she was taking at her church on the value of a personal testimony. At the end of the lesson, the leader suggested that everyone prepare his or her own story of Jesus' saving work, and come back the following week ready to share it. Veronica found this an exciting challenge, because since first hearing about Jesus, she had been forgiven her sins and healed of a painful physical complaint. Also, with God's help, she had given up both smoking and drinking to which she had been addicted. Writing down her testimony would be a great reminder of what God had done for her, especially as she would have a more complete story to share with Sam, her husband, who had only heard parts of it.

While the apostle Paul's times in prison may have seemed an enormous hindrance to his work, they provided this pioneer missionary with many extra opportunities to tell the story of how Jesus had changed him. Indeed, so powerful was his testimony that King Agrippa found it very persuasive—and he was only listening to it in the context of a trial!

Many people have become Christians through hearing or reading about the way God has changed someone else. Who knows how Sam will respond when Veronica finds the right time to share her story? Having heard the gospel already, it may be just what he needs to remind him how much Veronica really has changed.

Suggested Prayer
Lord, please show me how I can weave what you have done for me into a compelling story that I can share with others ... especially my husband.

A Practical Suggestion
As a useful exercise, write out your testimony, commit the main points to memory, then ask one of your Christian friends if you can "practice" on them.

Putting Your Foot in It

How long will you keep getting drunk? 1 SAMUEL 1:14

Read: James 3:1-12

Eli, the Old Testament priest at Shiloh, probably felt a bit foolish after confronting Hannah at the temple with the accusation that she was drunk. When Hannah expressed her true condition—that she was in anguish before God because she had no son—Eli may have wished he could have retracted his hasty words. Not being able to bear children was a shameful burden for a Hebrew woman to carry in those days, and Eli understood immediately why she would be weeping before God.

We don't know what harm might have been done by Eli's inappropriate words. Hannah responded to the priest with characteristic grace, but his accusation may have added an additional burden of shame to her already burdened heart. When we speak out of turn, without thinking first, we very often hurt people, or cause them to respond indignantly, with anger or resentment.

Tanya was a young woman who often spoke without thinking. There were many events in her life she wished had never happened or that she could completely forget. In reality, though, the memories remained and sent cold shivers down her spine whenever she recalled them. One of the worst times was when she inadvertently asked the mailman an offensive question; another was when she got angry one Sunday and ended up shouting at the pastor on the church steps. Tanya recognized her failures and sought God for his help to tame her tongue. She asked him to do so in order that her witness in front of Derek, her husband, was not compromised so often. Instinctively she knew that if she could conquer this problem, he might become a Christian sooner.

Imperfect Christians, even though redeemed by God, still have the capacity to foul things up by what they say. If your deepest desire is to see your husband come to Christ, you will not want to ruin your witness at home by saying a lot of inappropriate things you'll later regret. Ask God to tame your tongue.

Suggested Prayer

Lord, I know that when my emotions are aroused I can say the most unfortunate things. With your help, I pray that I will be much more in control of myself so that I won't let you down by what I say.

A Practical Suggestion

Why not promise yourself and God that you will count to ten before you speak on occasions when you could become angry or when someone takes you by surprise?

With many ... words he pleaded with them. ACTS 2:40

Read: Acts 2:14-16; 36-41

Karen was on vacation with her family when they visited a wildlife park one day. After seeing the animals, birds, pet corner, adventure playground, and souvenir shop, they listened to the owner speak about the need for increased conservation of some species of birds and mammals. Karen was struck with this man's deep commitment to protect endangered species, and the passionate way he pleaded for immediate action on their behalf.

However, his dedication was not merely verbal. He had given up a well-paying job, sold his family's home, and taken out a bank loan in order to buy the land on which the wildlife park now stood. What is more, he was involved politically in trying to get certain practices stopped worldwide that have been destroying the habitat of many endangered species. Yet, despite his words, it was his passionate pleas to the audience to help in this work of conservation that affected Karen most. She wondered how many more people, including her own husband, Joe, would be Christians by now if she and other Christians were as deeply passionate for Christ and his work of mission.

On the Day of Pentecost it was not only the words Peter spoke, but also his passionate pleading that led to the conversion of three thousand people. Today we need more Christians with a greater passion to see others of their family and friends brought to Christ.

Suggested Prayer
Lord, please give me a real burden to see my family and friends come to you so that I do more to help bring them to you.

A Practical Suggestion
If you would feel uncomfortable pleading with someone to become a Christian, practice first on a doll or a stuffed animal to see what it feels like to appeal to someone in this way.

Wives should submit to their husbands in everything. Ephesians 5:24

Read: Ephesians 5:21—6:4

Throughout our modern world, human beings are taught to relate to one another by mutual agreement and compromise more than by domination and obedience. Indeed, it may only be in animal training classes that the term "obedience" is commonplace. It certainly surprised Geraldine when, having recently become a Christian, she heard these verses from Ephesians 5 being read in church. When she married Tom she did not promise in the vows to obey him. She thought the concept of obeying your husband had gone out with the Dark Ages!

However, Christians believe that the Bible is God's revealed truth and should therefore form the basis of all that they are taught. What is more, many Christians realize that they should not attempt to simply fill their minds with this truth, but that it should govern their lifestyle too. This is what worried Geraldine. She was not sure what this biblical teaching on submission meant for her, since she was married to an unbeliever. How could she submit to Tom without compromising her faith?

As she discussed her concern with her friends at church, Geraldine understood better that God himself demands her greatest love and loyalty. She also realized that he encourages her to fully commit herself to her marriage unless and until her husband makes demands of her that contradict her faith. True, she may have to cope with personal sacrifice sometimes, such as missing church because of his wishes. However, her goal is to love, honor, and respect Tom, so that he will see Jesus Christ in her and respond to God's call himself.

Suggested Prayer
Desiring more than anything, Lord, that my husband find you, I pray for your grace and love to live such a compelling life as a Christian that he will want to love and trust you too. Please help him to notice Jesus in me!

A Question to Answer
Do you have any irritating habits your husband has complained about that you'd be willing to change in order to show your love for him?

Getting It Right

"I know that the Lord has given this land to you." JOSHUA 2:9

Read: Joshua 2:1-14

"Where should my ultimate loyalty lie?" That was a question Jane asked herself every day. Her specific and long-term goal was that Dave, her husband of seven years, should become a Christian, as she had done three years earlier. In the short term, when Dave wanted to go out for the day on Sundays, she agreed, but only reluctantly. She would much rather have been at church and always felt guilty for being absent. Deep down Jane was totally committed both to her marriage and to God, but she felt torn nevertheless.

The biblical account of Rahab's faith was a source of inspiration to Jane. Rahab lived in Jericho, a city that God intended to be taken by his Israelite people. The book of Hebrews tells us that her faith in God was so strong she believed the prediction of the Israelite spies and cooperated fully with them. Rahab's reward was not only to be saved when the city was destroyed, but also, after her death, to be included in the catalog of people who have demonstrated great faith in God (Heb 11:31).

Rahab discerned that the eternal dimension is ultimately the most important. Jane, and other wives in her situation, have to make their own decisions as to what to do when there is a conflict between their short-term and long-term priorities, but the same God is there to guide them as guided Rahab.

Suggested Prayer

When I find it hard to make decisions, Lord, help me to sense what is right for the present situation, and what course to take that will ultimately help bring about your long-term plans for my husband and me.

A Question to Answer

Have you ever specifically asked God to show you what his long-term plans are for your life? If not, ask him now.

God's Strength in Our Weakness 39

When I am weak, then I am strong. 2 CORINTHIANS 12:10

Read: 2 Corinthians 12:1-10

Avery felt particularly despondent as she sat in her armchair by the fire. When she married Brian over twenty years earlier they were both committed and enthusiastic Christians. However, it was now well over a decade that she'd been going to church alone. Brian no longer had any personal faith in God, and, due partly to his feelings of guilt, their relationship became strained whenever they attempted to discuss anything to do with Christianity or church. Avery had suffered years of sadness over her situation and now felt completely drained. What she needed more than anything was God's reassurance.

God's apostle Paul felt low at times too. On one occasion he pleaded with God to remove a problem from his life, but instead of answering the prayer as Paul expected, God told him that whenever he was feeling weak, inadequate, or vulnerable, he was potentially in a position of enormous strength. Paul learned from experience that Christians at their weakest and lowest are prime candidates to receive huge injections of God's energy and power.

Many Christians feel sad over a painful situation at home. Like Avery, they sense they are getting nowhere and can't see any light at the end of the tunnel. God wants to encourage Avery, and others like her, as he did Paul.

Do you ever feel so weak in your situation that you're not sure you can go on? God's word to you today is to abandon whatever resources you feel you have left and open yourself to him. He can transform your future, filling you with his power, hope, and vision. Then you will be able to cope—whatever happens.

Suggested Prayer
When I feel despondent, Lord, I often lose faith in what you can do. Forgive me, I pray, and help me surrender my weakness to you so that you can fill me again with your dynamic power.

A Practical Suggestion

List all the things that God may see as a hindrance to his working in your life. Pray through each one, asking God to take away all that is unhelpful, and then invite him to give you a fresh injection of his power.

Other seed fell on good soil. It came up, grew and produced a crop.
MARK 4:8

Read: Mark 4:1-20

Rhonda found her mind wandering as the discussion at her Bible study group continued around her. During a series of studies on Jesus' parables, the group was now looking at Jesus' story of the sower, and considering the different kinds of soil on which the seed fell. As each one was discussed, Rhonda tried to identify which was the nearest to Alex, her husband, who, while still an unbeliever, attended church more often now. This meant that he was having the seed of the gospel sown into his mind quite frequently. What was preoccupying Rhonda was the question of whether she could help change the "soil" of Alex's life into the "good soil" that produced "a crop."

Did Alex represent the path where Satan "takes away the word that was sown" (v. 15)? Was he more like the "rocky places" where the word is received with joy, but then abandoned when difficulties arise (vv. 5-6; 16-17)? Maybe Alex was like the thorns where worldly concerns and other priorities swamp any emerging life in the new plant (vv. 7; 18-19)? Rhonda struggled to categorize Alex, but promised herself and God that she would pray for discernment in the next few days.

The conclusion she reached about Alex is between her and God. The benefit to Rhonda in praying this through is that she can now pray more specifically for her husband, and pray against whatever distractions are hindering his becoming "good soil"—which is the point at which he will make a genuine, deep, and informed commitment of his life to Jesus.

Suggested Prayer
Please give me, Lord, that ability to see and understand what is hindering my husband from coming to faith in Jesus. Then show me what to pray for and against.

A Question to Answer
Is God calling you to do anything that would make it easier for your husband to commit his life to Jesus?

A Risky Choice

Jonah ran away from the Lord. JONAH 1:3

Read: Jonah 1:1-17

Stephanie had had about as much as she could take and was ready to run away from home. She and Bob had just had another major fight over money. No matter how much they talked and argued about it, they couldn't seem to agree on how to spend it. Bob prided himself on his financial management skills and had kept a tight rein on their finances over the years. They certainly did not lack for material things, and Stephanie was not ungrateful, but she wished for more say in how to spend their money. Being a Christian, she longed to give more to various ministries and charities, rather than buying more expensive cars and vacations for themselves, but Bob just couldn't see it. His heart was far more fixed on making sure they were comfortable now, as well as being materially set for the future.

His plans for their future, however, had suffered a major setback. His business had recently run into big trouble, and finances at home had to be severely curtailed. Any money to charity was first on his list of items to slash. Even though he couldn't understand Stephanie's "obsession" with the church, he had never complained about the money she faithfully dropped in the offering plate each week ... until now.

"They've got you brainwashed, Stephanie!" Bob was shouting. "Don't you know they just spend all that money on bigger and better church buildings? We can't keep throwing away our money like that anymore. It's got to stop!"

This was the last straw for Stephanie. She had prayed and prayed for Bob over the years, and yet he remained hardened to God and had little real concern for anyone but himself. *Lord, I just can't do this anymore,* she prayed desperately. *Bob will never change and I can't stay here one more day. I do love him, but we're just such different people.* Without answering Bob's tirade, Stephanie ran into the bedroom and slammed the door. She decided the next time she came out would be to say good-bye.

Centuries ago the prophet Jonah also felt he couldn't do what God was asking of him. He had been called by God to tell the wicked city of Ninevah about God's mercy and love for them, but they were such wicked people Jonah was sure they didn't *deserve* God's mercy. And he wasn't about to be the one to tell them—which is why he ran as fast as he could in the opposite direction. We have only to see the extraordinary lengths God went to in using a big fish to swallow Jonah to understand that God does not take kindly to missionaries who abandon their calling.

If Stephanie is not to become a modern-day Jonah, she needs support, prayer, and plenty of encouragement from Christian friends. Do you have a friend who wants to run away from her calling of being a missionary in her own home? Or have you yourself contemplated giving up on the challenges in your life? God is calling you to be his witness—in your home, your church, your workplace—and to encourage others in difficult circumstances.

Suggested Prayer

Father, I know you have put me in my home with a special missionary task to fulfill. Please strengthen me and remind me of my calling whenever I am tempted to give up and take an easier path.

A Question to Answer

Before you give up on God's calling to you at home, have you stopped to consider everything he has ever done for you from the moment of your conception until today?

The Pain of Trial

"Take your son, your only son ... sacrifice him." GENESIS 22:2

Read: Genesis 22:1-14

Abraham's trial was supremely painful. It's difficult to even imagine what God had asked of him: to sacrifice the son he knew had been a special gift from God. Abraham was certain that God's promise to make him the father of "a great nation" (Gn 12:2) would be fulfilled through Isaac. Therefore, he could see no logic in God's instruction to sacrifice his son, but because he trusted God, he made plans to do the unthinkable. He believed God would not fail him ... and he did not.

Nicole was also given a difficult trial in her life. Even though she was glad to be a Christian, and her life now had much more meaning than before, she carried a deep pain inside because her husband, Ian, did not share her faith. What was more, she had reason to believe that after seventeen years of marriage, he was cheating on her. The day eventually came when her suspicions were confirmed. Ian confessed his long-standing affair with a co-worker from the office and asked Nicole for a divorce.

The pain of his betrayal tore Nicole apart. She had so hoped that her prayers for him would be answered soon. She still loved him very much, and the thought of his spending eternity without God had weighed on her mind night and day. But divorce wasn't something she had ever considered ... not even for a moment.

Nicole certainly faced a difficult test of faith. Like Abraham, she felt confused and not able to understand what God was asking of her in this situation. She took comfort, however, in this story of Abraham, who chose to believe in God's goodness and provision even in the face of his greatest trial. Nicole's closest Christian friends stood with her in prayer and gave her the emotional support she needed to face her trial with courage. She determined in her heart to receive this situation as an opportunity to expect God to work a miracle and to bring good out of the confusion and pain.

Suggested Prayer

Heavenly Father, help me not to resent the hard parts of my Christian life, or to lose my faith when difficult times come. You are my strong pillar, Lord ... a firm foundation ... and I choose to lean on you and believe that you can bring good out of the most painful situations and trials.

A Practical Suggestion

Think of a trial you have faced. What good things did God bring out of those difficult circumstances? If you are facing a painful trial right now, what good things can you imagine God accomplishing? Write them down with today's date, then start making a list of God's answers to prayer, large or small, when they happen. They may not be what you expect, but they will come.

More Than We Can Imagine

You have saved the best till now. JOHN 2:10

Read: John 2:1-11

Sometimes Jesus surprises us. At the wedding in Cana, he took an intriguing course of action, preventing a catastrophe at what was meant to be a celebration. Had he not done so, the family whose wedding it was would have inherited a negative reputation in the community for running out of wine. Jesus' miracle saved the day and completely transformed the situation.

Jesus acted in an unpredictable way at that wedding; no one could have guessed what he would do. It was often like this during his three years of public ministry. People could never tell whose life would be the next to be revolutionized.

Jeanne is a young wife and mother who is waiting for Jesus to revolutionize her life. She often wonders how much longer her present nightmare will last. Despite some moments of peace at home, there are many times when, for no obvious reason, trouble flares. According to her husband, Sam, Jeanne's friends from church are to blame for everything, but she knows this isn't true. Sam is using her church friends as an excuse to avoid dealing with his real problems. Jeanne worries about their two young children and how the extreme tension in their home is going to affect them. She is praying for Jesus somehow to intervene, to hold their marriage together and bring peace to their lives.

It could be that Jesus will surprise Jeanne and bring about a solution she cannot begin to imagine. In his letter to the Ephesians, the apostle Paul acknowledges that God's answers will often surprise us. God "is able to do immeasurably more than all we ask or imagine ..." (3:20). By his grace and power, Jesus loves to surprise people who trust him. His call to Jeanne, and others like her, is to keep trusting, keep praying—and wait. He can turn her nightmare into a celebration.

Suggested Prayer

While I would be so thrilled if my husband became a Christian today, Lord, I recognize that this miracle will not happen according to my timetable, but yours. Strengthen me so that I can remain faithful to you while I wait.

A Practical Suggestion

When you next go to church, as you sing, pray, and listen to God's Word, count up the number of rich expressions of love God has already given you.

                 God's Promised Presence

The angel went to her and said ... "The Lord is with you." LUKE 1:28

Read: Luke 1:26-38

Eva was desperate. After twenty-six years of marriage, all but one of them as a Christian, she had lost any hope that Henry would ever share her faith. He seemed as resistant now as ever. Indeed, his cynicism about all religions had never abated, despite seeing Eva gradually transformed from the nervous, hesitant girl he had married into the gentle but confident wife and mother she was now. He seemed to think there was no link between her faith and her growing self-confidence. She knew otherwise.

Eva continued her daily prayers for Henry, but it was more out of a sense of duty than belief that the man she loved would be changed by the risen Christ. Then one day, as she prayed, something unique happened. She felt a warm glow and sensed in a new way the reassuring and peaceful presence of Jesus. Joy surged up within her and she praised God, realizing that he was meeting her where she was, and letting her know that he was listening to her prayers. She was not alone with her pain.

The Bible tells of numerous occasions when desperate people called to God and he responded in a tangible way. With a unique calling ahead of her, Mary received the message of reassurance brought to her by God's angel. Throughout history, people have testified how God has broken into their lives in unusual and tangible ways to give fresh hope and the promise of his future presence. Who knows how he may work next in your life?

Suggested Prayer
I am very open to you, Lord, if you want to break into my life to say or share anything. Help me to be receptive to anything you want to say to me, in whatever way you choose.

A Practical Suggestion
Make sure you do not spend all of your prayer time talking to God. Take time to be quiet and still. Then listen carefully.

God's Rich Love

How beautiful you are, my darling! Oh, how beautiful.
SONG OF SOLOMON 1:15

Read: Song of Solomon 1:1-17

Charlene never quite knew how to respond to her friends at work, and even a few at church, who complained constantly about their marriages. She almost felt guilty for being so happy with her husband, Sean. They had first been attracted to each other because they shared similar interests, and their personalities were compatible enough that they rarely disagreed about anything important. They had a healthy respect for each other, made time to talk, and planned regular date nights. After seven years of marriage they were at least as passionately in love as they had been when they were courting.

The only major issue that divided Charlene and Sean was her faith. She had become a Christian shortly after their fourth wedding anniversary, but while Sean had examined Christianity, he was reluctant to commit himself. They never argued about Charlene's faith. Sean wasn't opposed to it; he just felt he needed more time before making a commitment. Despite this difference, she and Sean were genuinely happy together. When a few of her church friends questioned how she could be truly happy married to an unbeliever, she began to wonder how God felt about their love for each other.

She mentioned this to her pastor, and he suggested she read Song of Solomon. At first she found it hard to believe that so much romantic love was expressed in the Bible. However, she felt God reassure her that love was his gift to people to share and enjoy in this life, even those who did not yet know him. Charlene also felt a renewed call to pray that Sean would soon come to see love not merely as a human phenomenon, but as a gift from God, who *is* love. As for her friends, Charlene decided to stop feeling guilty and to thank God every day for the precious gift of love he had given her and Sean.

Suggested Prayer

I pray that you will help me appreciate the love I share with my husband, Lord. Show me how we can encourage it to grow and deepen even more.

A Practical Suggestion

Set some time aside and make the necessary arrangements for a surprise date with your husband, doing something you both enjoy.

"Were not all ten cleansed? Where are the other nine?" LUKE 17:17

Read: Luke 17:11-19

Jesus didn't get it. He had just healed ten men of leprosy and they had excitedly run off to see a priest, who would confirm their miraculous healing from the dreaded disease. All ten men had pleaded with Jesus to heal them and he had done so. But only one man—a foreigner, no less—had taken the time and trouble to come back and thank him. This perplexed Jesus, who wondered aloud why the other men were not grateful.

Pauline didn't get it either when it came to her husband, Trevor. Her Christian faith meant so much to her that she simply couldn't understand Trevor's complacent attitude. To her, sin, repentance, forgiveness, and trusting Jesus for spiritual guidance all made so much sense. Trevor considered Christianity "a fairy tale," and with his Catholic upbringing, he said he'd had enough of that nonsense as a child. He encouraged Pauline to go to church if it "did her some good" but was totally unenthusiastic about doing so himself. Pauline was so grateful to God for all of his wonderful blessings that she couldn't understand why Trevor just didn't seem to care.

Other people's behavior will confuse us at times because we can't see into their minds and hearts. Pauline may never understand why Trevor cannot grasp what is so obvious to her. Even Jesus was amazed by the ungrateful lepers, but that did not stop his continuing to reach out and minister to people. We may be bewildered, but we can continue to pray.

Suggested Prayer

Lord, when the behavior of other people baffles me, help me to keep my eyes primarily on you, because I know you act consistently for my good.

A Practical Suggestion

To ensure that you do not take Jesus and his love for granted, make a list of at least ten things he has done for you and your family, and for which you are grateful … and thank him right now!

When the Lord saw that he had gone over to look, God called to him.
EXODUS 3:4

Read: Exodus 3:1-10

God had a special and unique task for Moses to do. He was to represent God before Pharaoh, king of Egypt, and speak what God wanted him to say. The problem was that God did not yet have Moses' attention, which meant that Moses was not yet attuned to his voice. God needed to attract his attention before he could communicate anything, and on this unique occasion, he opted to use a flaming bush that did not burn up.

Alexandra did not expect to find a flaming bush in her life, but she believed that God would guide her somehow. She found it difficult to know how forward she should be with her husband, Kevin, and his family in sharing the gospel with them. None of them believed in Jesus as she did. She knew, of course, that Jesus' mandate for all Christians is to go and make disciples (Mt 28:19), but when it came to how and when she should do this with Kevin, she was uncertain. She wondered if she should come home from church every Sunday and tell him what it had been about, or whether she should tell him about her daily Bible study and prayer time on the days when it was especially inspiring. This is why she had asked God for his help; she wanted him to guide her.

God's way of guiding Alexandra will be suited to her life and needs. He speaks to people today in a variety of ways. This includes counsel from other Christians, as well as directly from the Holy Spirit as we read the Bible and pray. What is certain is that by one means or another God will guide Alexandra just as surely as he led Moses.

Suggested Prayer
Father, when I am not sure what kind of approach or strategy is best in my situation at home, please show me your way.

A Question to Answer

How many different ways can you think of that you have experienced God speaking to you since you became a Christian? Ask some of your Christian friends how they have experienced God's guidance in their lives.

Living in an Unfair World

*Stephen, full of the Holy Spirit, looked up to heaven
and saw the glory of God.* ACTS 7:55

Read: Acts 6:8-15; 7:51-60

Lynn was strangely quiet during her home fellowship meeting. When the group of seven women first began to meet about five years earlier, only one of them had a Christian husband. Now Hillary's husband, Josh, had committed his life to Jesus the previous weekend. Hillary was exuberant, and everyone was elated, except Lynn, who, while trying to smile, felt strangely isolated. This group had committed itself to praying these six men into God's kingdom. Now five had responded; God was answering their prayers. *I should be happier for Hillary,* Lynn chided herself. *What on earth is the matter with me?*

Lynn found herself struggling with a number of conflicting feelings. She wanted to be happy for Hillary and share her joy, but she was worried that now the group would concentrate mainly on providing mutual support for the women whose husbands were new Christians. She couldn't help thinking that she would feel left out. Then a sudden surge of anger welled up inside. It was not fair … she didn't deserve this! It was not her fault that Terry, her husband, was not remotely interested in her faith.

Stephen's martyrdom was grossly unfair too—far more so, of course, than Lynn's situation. What Stephen found was that God compensated him in a wonderfully rich way for his human disadvantage. He was given a glimpse into heaven itself—something very unusual, and hardly what Lynn could expect. However, in his own way and out of his love, God may well have special encouragements for Lynn. He certainly does not want her to feel isolated.

Suggested Prayer

Help me, Lord, when I feel discouraged and isolated … or if I find I am disadvantaged through no obvious fault of my own. Give me new strength to cope.

A Question to Answer

Let's shift the focus from you to someone you know. Can you think of any of your friends who may feel disadvantaged for reasons not of their own making? If so, pray for them and see if there is anything practical you can do to help and encourage them.

Keep on speaking. ACTS 18:9

Read: Acts 18:1-11

Debbie felt that God was urging her to witness occasionally, yet positively, about her faith to her husband, Luke, and she did. She was careful to pick her moments, but when the right occasion came, she told him what Jesus meant to her. She explained how he wanted to bless their marriage, how he answered her prayers, and what a lot of joy she got from being part of the church. She was careful always to work out in advance what she would tell Luke, and was sensitive, avoiding comments that might appear critical of him or their marriage. She wanted to encourage the man she loved, not deflate him or drive him further from Christ.

Luke's reaction to Debbie's testimony varied. Sometimes he listened; at other times he stopped her midway. It seemed that his mood determined how much he could cope with. Even when he stopped Debbie, he was not intentionally unkind, although sometimes she felt frustrated.

The apostle Paul must have felt frustrated too when the Jews at Corinth rejected his message. God's words to him in a vision one night must have given him renewed confidence that he was doing the right thing. Certainly God wants us to keep on telling others about his love and grace. Our task is to remain faithful, and we should talk sensitively about his love to those who do not know him personally. Debbie must not give up, but she needs to pick her moments as carefully as possible.

Suggested Prayer
Give me the confidence and boldness I need to speak out for you, Lord. Guide me as to when I should speak and when I should remain silent. Let my words bear fruit for your kingdom.

A Practical Suggestion
When you feel that God is calling you to witness for him, if you have advance warning, pray through and plan in your mind (and maybe on paper) the sort of things you want to say. Then when the time comes, quietly ask God to guide every word you speak.

They received their sight and followed him. MATTHEW 20:34

Read: Matthew 20:29-34

When Jesus was engaged in ministry on earth, he healed many blind eyes. People who had lived their lives in blackness, or whose sight was severely impaired, suddenly found, with a touch from Jesus, that the shapes separated and the colors became distinguishable. Life could now be lived as God intended instead of trying to negotiate the many hazards with which visually impaired people have to cope.

Annie knew what it was to be spiritually blind, and to be touched by Jesus and made whole. Two years earlier, after her friend Sylvia had told her about Jesus for the umpteenth time, suddenly it had made sense to her. It was as if someone had turned the lights on. She stepped from the darkness of spiritual blindness into the glorious light of Jesus. Now she understood why Christians get excited about Jesus, and as she grew in her faith, she began praying constantly for her husband Roger's conversion, praying that the light would be switched on for him too.

Annie had the faith to believe Jesus can heal physically blind eyes, so why should he not open spiritually blind eyes? Why should Jesus not do for Roger what he had already done for her?

It was this spiritual logic that prompted Annie to commit herself to praying more intently than ever before for Roger. One day, Roger may be more grateful for this than words can express.

Suggested Prayer

Lord Jesus, please help me to be faithful to you, whatever you ask of me, so that others may be brought from darkness into your light. Keep stimulating and encouraging my faith so that my life will glorify your name.

A Practical Suggestion

Consider making a covenant with God that you will pray daily for your husband to come to faith—until he does. Put your commitment on paper, sign it, and date it to show that you are serious.

51

If we confess our sins, he ... will forgive us our sins. 1 JOHN 1:9

Read: 1 John 1:5—2:2

Jocelyn had been a Christian for over two decades before she realized she had some unfinished business with God. She had grown up in a Christian family, had made a personal commitment to Christ at age ten, but then went through a spiritually lean period in her later teens. At twenty-one she recommitted her life to the Lord, and two years later met Gary. He was not a believer, but she quickly fell in love with his engaging personality, and dismissed any reservations she had over his lack of faith. After a whirlwind courtship, they married and settled into a comfortable life. Gary was sympathetic to Jocelyn's faith and he supported her, but never committed his own life to Christ.

Jocelyn spent years trying to prove to her Christian friends that she was at no disadvantage being married to someone who did not share her faith. But deep down, she knew that her relationship with Gary was lacking, and she found herself jealous of friends who could pray with their husbands, read the Bible together, and go to church as a family. She was unable to share the most important part of her life with Gary. At the time of their marriage, she had rationalized that passages like Deuteronomy 7:3-4 and 2 Corinthians 6:14-16 did not apply to her. Gary was such a "good" man and would make a wonderful husband in every other way, she had told herself. Besides, didn't 1 Corinthians 7:14 teach that her husband would somehow become "sanctified" through her?

It was only after many years of living with an unbeliever that she understood the wisdom of the scriptural warnings against spiritually mixed marriages. Engaged in a Bible study with some Christian women friends, she saw that God has warned believers not to become involved in such a marriage in the first place—and certainly not with any thought that by getting married, a believing partner will help the other come to faith. It may happen, but it is far more likely that the spiritual life of the believer will suffer, often seriously.

Recognizing her earlier pride, rebellion, and disobedience, Jocelyn repented humbly and sincerely before God. It was her thirtieth birthday, and the gift of forgiveness she received was better than any other present! As for her marriage, Jocelyn continues to pray for Gary every day, and asks for God to help her stay strong in her faith.

Suggested Prayer

Where I have been disobedient, Lord, please forgive me as I confess my sin. Then use me for your glory as never before, especially to help my husband find you.

A Question to Answer

Do you believe Jesus can forgive you for *anything* you have done, thought, or said wrongly? He can—and wants to!

Gaining Fresh Hope

I will bring health and healing. JEREMIAH 33:6

Read: Jeremiah 33:1-16

If you looked at Gloria, you would probably never know how hard she found life. In fact, behind her front door, things were very difficult for her and her partner, Sam. They had lived together for many years when Gloria was led to Christ by a friend at work. Gradually, as she grew in faith, she felt that God wanted her unhappy life to improve. Gloria and Sam had always argued a lot but had remained together. Increasingly Gloria sensed that this was not normal; nor was it right for them to share a home and bed without being married. She was desperate to see things change, yet Sam was unresponsive when she tried to talk with him. Despite her dilemma, Gloria had a deep assurance that God knew about her situation, loved her, and ultimately would work things out for her and Sam. That made a lot of difference.

Jeremiah had an incredibly difficult situation to live with too. Jerusalem was under siege, the people were disillusioned, Jeremiah himself was in prison, and he knew things would get much worse before God's promises of healing, forgiveness, and restoration came to pass. Despite this, he was able to cope with his present pain because he knew God was going to work powerfully in the future.

God still gives hope in situations where darkness seems to reign, but, like Jeremiah, we can open ourselves to hear God's word of hope—and then believe it!

Suggested Prayer
Father, help me to catch a vision of your future plans. Show me a glimpse of what you can do—especially in my husband's life.

A Question to Answer
Have you read any section of the Bible recently that describes God's great power and strength? If not, it could be a good use of some time today! Read one or two of the psalms that speak of God's majesty.

The winds blew and beat against that house; yet it did not fall.
MATTHEW 7:25

Read: Matthew 7:24-29

The biggest concern Josie had was that her three young children—Sophie, Rachel, and Adam—would not hear much about Jesus during their formative years. David, her husband, was not especially anti-Christian, but he didn't like the idea of Josie "brainwashing" the children with her Christian beliefs. No one should be indoctrinated about what to believe, he insisted, and just as he and Josie had had the opportunity to make up their own mind about Christianity, so should their children.

Josie, however, was less than certain that such a policy was a responsible one. She opposed indoctrination too, but felt it was her duty as a Christian parent, albeit a new one, to teach her children who Jesus was, and what he offers to people who trust him. She couldn't believe this would do them any harm; on the contrary, it would provide them with the firmest foundation of all on which to built their future lives.

Jesus clearly taught that the only way to live a fulfilled and stable life is to base our lives on him and his teaching. Only if we build on that sure foundation alone will we have God's strength within us and be able to withstand the storms that afflict us.

Suggested Prayer
Lord, please help me to live the kind of secure life that Jesus promised. Then help others, especially my family, to see in me how fulfilling and worthwhile it is to trust you.

A Question to Answer
As you reflect on your life since you became a Christian, what differences can you see in yourself that indicate what God has done for you? Thank God for all the good things you have seen.

54

Jesus ... called to him those he wanted, and they came to him. MARK 3:13

Read: Mark 3:13-19

No matter what she did, Brenda could not persuade Joe to have anything to do with her church. Every time she tried to get him to join her, he reminded her that when he was taken as a child, the church was full of little children and old ladies with old-fashioned hats and smelly perfume. Men were a rare sight—apart from the pastor, of course—and he spoke in a strange singsong voice that Joe deemed utterly false. If this was Christianity, he had decided long ago that he wanted nothing to do with it.

Brenda knew she had an uphill struggle. Her goal was to help Joe see how much of a man's man Jesus was. There was nothing effeminate about him; in order to prepare for the continuance of his work once he had completed his role on earth and returned to heaven, he chose a group of men who were among the toughest and most strong-willed around to share in his ministry. In no way did he exclude women from his life, but he opted to share with men the specific task of developing on earth the work he had begun.

Convincing Joe to look at Christianity in a different light was never going to be easy for Brenda. She resolved, however, to show him, little by little, that the most masculine man of all, and one well worth following, was the one Joe was refusing to acknowledge.

Suggested Prayer

Father, help me to show my husband and other people I know who do not yet believe in Jesus what kind of person he really is ... so their response to him will be based on accurate information.

A Practical Suggestion

Without undue pressure, see if you can arrange for your husband to meet some men from your church in a relaxed social environment—perhaps attending a sporting event, or joining in a church baseball league or bowling team.

As long as Moses held up his hands, the Israelites were winning.
EXODUS 17:11

Read: Exodus 17:8-16

Gail listened intently to the message her pastor was giving to kick off the church's new Prayer Thrust:

"So Moses raised his hands in the wilderness," the pastor concluded, "to commend symbolically to God the battle against the Amalekites in the valley below. And God honored him. In the same way God continues to respond to heartfelt prayers brought to him by those who sincerely want him to be glorified on earth."

Gail felt deeply challenged by the pastor's message and the call to pick a specific need she had, then pray about it with greater intensity than ever before. The church's "Prayer Thrust" had been introduced to stimulate more praying by the fellowship, and Gail promptly committed herself to pray with renewed faith for Phil, her husband, who showed only slight interest in anything spiritual. She really believed that within a week she would see a noticeable change.

However, two weeks later nothing had happened. Phil seemed totally unchanged, and Gail's faith was beginning to waver. Phil was still as helpful as ever around the house but showed no more interest than before in God. She expressed her disappointment to her friend Kathy, who reminded her that God has his own timetable, which we neither know nor understand. Kathy encouraged Gail to remember that we are engaged in a spiritual battle for others' souls, and the battle may be long and hard as we face resistance from the enemy of our souls. But we can know with certainty that the battle is already won, the enemy already defeated by Christ's death on the cross, and we can keep trusting that God will honor our prayers.

After this, Gail continued to pray for Phil just as passionately as before, but now she was prepared to wait for God to answer in his own time. Her role was to pray faithfully, however long it took. Interestingly, she sensed that as she prayed daily for Phil, she was being drawn closer to both him and God.

Suggested Prayer

Please help me, Lord, to be one of your most faithful and determined prayer warriors as I regularly commit to you my family, and especially my husband, in the spiritual battle for their souls.

A Practical Suggestion

If you struggle to pray as consistently as you would like, try a little "battle strategy": look at your whole day and decide what time and place will be the best for devoting yourself to prayer. Write yourself a reminder and post it where you'll be sure to see it. When the time comes, take your phone off the hook and go for it!

The Permanence of Marriage

They will become one flesh. GENESIS 2:24

Read: Genesis 2:18-25

Geraldine was devastated when she arrived at the front door of the parsonage to speak with her pastor's wife, Renee. Gently, Renee helped her inside and patiently waited for Geraldine to calm down enough to spill out her story. For the past several months, Geraldine explained, she had been slightly suspicious that something unusual was going on, but she never seriously thought that Robert, her husband of eight years, would betray her. She had confronted him after dinner and had refused to accept his evasive answers. To her horror, he finally confessed that for a year now he'd been having an affair with a family friend. Having heard as much as she could cope with, Geraldine had rushed for the door and come straight here to pour out her pain.

With Renee's reassuring manner and sensitive help, Geraldine began to gain control of her emotions, and it was not long before she asked Renee whether she ought to seek a divorce. Renee refused to tell her specifically what to do, but wanted Geraldine to understand that biblically Robert's actions were grounds for divorce. Yet it could be that Robert, who had often been to church but never made a profession of faith, might repent and ask Geraldine to give him another chance.

Renee reminded Geraldine how God sees marriage as permanent, although he allows for divorce in cases of infidelity because, sadly, people are not always able to keep their promises. She showed Geraldine that if Robert were to repent, and she still loved him and could forgive him, God would be glad and would help to restore their relationship. Despite Robert's serious indiscretion, God still regarded them as one.

Suggested Prayer
Dear Lord, please help me to forgive if I have been hurt and sinned against. Heal my painful wounds and fill me with your extraordinary love.

A Question to Answer
Have you ever thought about how much God loves you and to what extent he has forgiven you? Sit and think about it now.

57 *The Remarkable Plans of God*

Joseph, the husband of Mary, of whom was born Jesus. MATTHEW 1:16

Read: Matthew 1:1-17

The beginning of Matthew's Gospel helps us to see things in perspective. For the benefit of his Jewish readers, Matthew detailed the way God so ordered the life of his Jewish people that a direct family line linked Abraham, through David, to Jesus, "who is called Christ." Matthew's purpose in cataloging what some might perceive as the most boring part of the New Testament was that we can see how, for century after century and in generation after generation, God worked out the plans he conceived before time began. It is a great comfort to know that God is still working out his eternal plans for the world and for each one of us.

First Timothy tells us that God "wants all men to be saved and to come to a knowledge of the truth" (2:4). We naturally would like to see all of our loved ones come into his kingdom, and it is clearly according to God's will for us to pray to this end. It is also not unusual for us, with our limited viewpoint, to be concerned that we can't always see the progress being made here and now in our lives. However, at the end of the day, while wanting God to bring many more people into his kingdom, we can do no more than trust, pray, and cooperate with God in any way he asks. Only he can fulfill his plans, and he does so according to his own timetable.

Suggested Prayer
Father, help me to trust you even when I don't understand what seems to be happening. Please remind me that your perspective is eternal, while mine is earthly and limited. Only you know what is for the best, Lord, and I will trust you.

A Question to Answer
If God was able to organize it so that his Son Jesus was born in just the right place to the right people at the right time, and in fulfillment of hundreds of earlier prophecies, do you not think he can work in your loved ones' lives?

He invited Philip to come up and sit with him. ACTS 8:31

Read: Acts 8:26-40

You could have knocked Barbara down with a feather! She and Steve had been married four years, during which time she had begun to follow Jesus. This was never a problem to Steve, and he sometimes accompanied Barbara to special events held at the church she attended. However, as far as she was concerned, Steve's level of interest in religion in general, and Christianity in particular, was small. What she did not know was that while she was at work some days and he was at home alone, he was reading the Christian books she brought into the house. Gradually, Steve was being drawn closer, and one day he knelt beside their bed and committed his life to loving and serving Jesus. When, some weeks later, he plucked up enough courage to tell Barbara, she was more ecstatic than words can describe!

Like Barbara, Philip was astounded by the way God works. Philip would not have understood to begin with why he had to leave the spiritual revival in Samaria to go out into the desert. Yet it all started to make sense when the Ethiopian came by reading about the Suffering Servant but not understanding anything about him. Philip wasted no time in telling him, led the man to Christ, and baptized him in an oasis in the desert. Philip knew that this amazing conversion was a result of God's gentle work of preparation and had very little to do with him.

Who knows where God may work next?

Suggested Prayer
Lord, while I am tempted to try to take control of situations, help me to see that only when your Holy Spirit works in people's lives do they really begin to understand anything about you. Do something unexpected in my husband's life so that he might want to know more about you.

A Practical Suggestion
However frustrated you may be because it seems that your husband's spiritual progress is slow, or even nonexistent, try praying more—not manipulating more.

You are neither cold nor hot. REVELATION 3:15

Read: Revelation 3:14-22

If it weren't for her two children, Teresa probably would not bother going to church, but because they enjoyed Sunday school she felt obliged to take them. Once, about fifteen years earlier as a teenager, she had committed her life to Jesus Christ. She was truly on fire for the Lord then, excited to share the Good News with everyone she met. In college, studying for a nursing career, she stayed involved in campus fellowships and witnessed regularly to other students. As time went by, however, Teresa found herself fully devoted to a busy nursing career, as well as her marriage and children. Being a mother and a nurse was very demanding, since she had to work many different shifts, often overnight, then grab only enough sleep to make it through the next day. Church and Christian fellowship had gradually taken a backseat to her many responsibilities, until finally she had come to a place of really not caring all that much about her relationship with Jesus or his church. She was still a believer, but the fire had gone out.

One Sunday as she sat reluctantly in church, Teresa found herself compelled to really listen to the sermon. It was not that the preacher was especially eloquent; it was more that he had a conviction and passion which shone through in his message. His deep concern was that the church should penetrate the local community with the love of Jesus, but for that to happen, it would demand the wholehearted commitment of those who were already part of God's family. He challenged each individual Christian to consider where they stood before God and, if necessary, to repent and rededicate themselves to him.

Teresa began to reflect on how she had wasted what God had done earlier in her life. Her love for him was lukewarm, if that. Her husband, together with most of his family, and certainly their neighbors, had no concept of God's love for them at all. As God spoke to Teresa she began to cry, but she reaffirmed in church that day how she planned to be on fire for Jesus from then on.

Suggested Prayer

I recognize, Lord, that lukewarm Christians are only of limited use in your plans for this world. I repent before you if this is how I am. Move in my life by your Spirit so that I am on fire for you, then work in my husband too.

A Question to Answer

Have you ever thought about how Jesus must feel when those for whom he died gradually start to fall out of love with him and stray away?

Coping with the Trial

Do not be surprised at the painful trial you are suffering.
1 PETER 4:12

Read: 1 Peter 4:12-19

It took a Sunday evening sermon that she didn't want to hear to show Valerie that God had not abandoned her. Her weekend had been fraught with tension. She had struggled to cope with two of her children who were ill, then in the morning she had been stopped from attending church because her husband, Ted, had insisted on playing golf. He arrived home quite late in the afternoon. By then, she'd been dealing with cranky children all day and cleaning up after the two who were sick. She was exhausted, tense, and totally unprepared to go to church that evening, but Ted insisted she should go ... slipping in a snide remark about how it might make her easier to live with. She agreed, but only to get some peace and quiet.

For the past few weeks, Valerie had been feeling increasingly unhappy about her domestic situation. Ted was always making fun of her church and faith. She felt it was so unfair, as she did nothing knowingly to provoke him. One evening he was extremely sarcastic about her in front of their dinner guests, who were Valerie's friends from work, and she became especially angry.

The sermon in church that night focused on Jesus' death on the cross and how, from our human perspective, his immense sacrifice was totally unjust. Valerie began to see her situation in a new light. She was having to endure a trial—but a much less serious one than Jesus went through for her. By the time the sermon ended she saw that it was a privilege for any Christian to "participate in the sufferings of Christ" (1 Pt 4:13), and she went home with a new attitude and commitment.

Suggested Prayer

Father, help me to see my trials in perspective rather than becoming miserable when life gets hard. Show me how you could work positively in my husband's life.

A Practical Suggestion

In the next few days try to visit someone you know, maybe from your church, who is having a hard time, too. Ask God to let your visit be a great encouragement to that person.

His heart went out to her. LUKE 7:13

Read: Luke 7:11-17

Sharon had been married to Ron, her second husband, for two years. She had been widowed five years earlier when Mike had died suddenly from a heart attack. He was a dedicated Christian, and they, together with their three children, had been genuinely happy. However, the impact of his death had affected Sharon deeply, and she found that her faith began to slide as she gradually came to terms with what had happened.

It was while she was struggling to understand how a loving God could deprive her of her husband that she met Ron and fell in love. When they had been married for a while it began to dawn on Sharon what she was missing. Ron had only a shallow interest in Christianity, and as she recognized that their relationship lacked any spiritual dimension, she began to feel disillusioned.

When Jesus entered Nain and witnessed the cruel effects of separation by death, he felt compassion for the mother whose only son had died. However, Jesus did not merely empathize or attempt to console her, he used his extraordinary power to reunite the family as he raised the boy from the dead.

Jesus' heart goes out to Sharon too. He understands her pain— both over Mike's death and the lack of a spiritual relationship with Ron. What is more, he is committed to working with Sharon as her faith begins to grow again, and she starts to share the Good News of Jesus with Ron.

Suggested Prayer
Lord, please help me to grasp the truth that when I feel pain inside, you feel it too. Thank you for the understanding and support you give me, but also for your commitment to help reduce the pain.

A Practical Suggestion
Take some time to meditate on how Jesus perceives your present situation. Ask him to reveal to you how he feels. If you sense he is sad, ask him to minister strength, hope, and encouragement to you.

He received his sight and followed Jesus. MARK 10:52

Read: Mark 10:46-52

Jennifer had been unwell for so long she could hardly recall what it felt like to be free of pain and discomfort. Depression had overtaken her at times, but the first sign of encouragement came when her neighbor, Tania, invited her to a healing service at a nearby church. Jennifer had never thought about an answer to her problems lying anywhere other than in conventional medicine, but she was both desperate and intrigued, and joined Tania with an open mind. She was impressed by what she heard and, displaying small but genuine faith in God, went forward to be prayed for. The miracle was not instant, but over the next few days her pain lessened and her spirits lifted. Within a week she was like a different person. Everyone who saw her remarked on the transformation, especially her husband, Barry.

He had been highly skeptical of all faith and religion until then, but he could not deny the change in Jennifer's health and disposition. Not surprisingly, she was enthusiastic about the God who had radically altered her life and was excited to get to know him better. She thought Barry would feel the same way, but he was more cautious.

It is no great surprise that anyone whom Jesus heals opts to follow him, but it is always harder for those who look on, even though they may be amazed and impressed. Jennifer's role now is to gently encourage Barry, rather than condemn him because he is taking longer than her to trust Jesus.

Suggested Prayer
Help me, Lord, to follow Jesus faithfully but not put unreasonable pressure on my husband, which could drive him further from you. Please give me the wisdom I need.

A Question to Answer
To whatever extent Jesus has worked in your life so far, do you take time regularly to thank him for his goodness and love?

Yet when planted, it grows and becomes the largest of all garden plants.
MARK 4:32

Read: Mark 4:30-34

Despite the jubilant worship in her church, Judith was discouraged one Sunday as she had coffee afterward with some of her friends. Not many Sundays before, she had heard a sermon on evangelism and sensed strongly that God was calling her to talk about him to her husband, Gerald. In the following couple of weeks she had found two or three opportunities to do so, telling him simply but coherently who Jesus is and the difference he makes to life today. She even told him how she had become a Christian herself. Now, though, she was disappointed because it seemed to have made no difference to him at all.

Jesus' parable about the mustard seed is one of his simplest and shortest, but for people like Judith it is among the most encouraging. We take it for granted in the world of nature that plants grow gradually, taking years or even decades to reach a substantial size. Jesus taught that the remarkable seed which is the Good News of God's kingdom— tiny and apparently insignificant though it may seem—will grow ultimately to become both enormous and influential. From Jesus' own ministry and that of his disciples it has grown into the worldwide Christian church, which is now a part of virtually every nation on earth.

While we applaud Judith's desire to see Gerald become a Christian quickly, she may have to wait and pray for much longer before the seed of the gospel germinates and grows in him. Yet it is the most important thing in all the world she can do.

Suggested Prayer
Heavenly Father, I do not find it easy to be patient. Please keep me faithful to you and my husband until he responds to your love.

A Practical Suggestion
If you share the gospel with your husband but can only tell him a little part at a time, make a written note of the things you say so that, by referring to your list once in a while, you can be sure to include all the main ingredients of the gospel.

God's Unseen Forces

64

Those who are with us are more than those who are with them.
2 KINGS 6:16

Read: 2 Kings 6:8-23

Hannah was not pleased with her church. They were planning an evangelistic crusade, with particular emphasis on outreach to children, young people, and the elderly. Hannah felt there was a large group being ignored—a group that included her own husband, Josh, and other men whose wives were part of the church, but who were unbelievers themselves. Nothing at all was being arranged to reach them, so armed with a constructive list of possible ideas, Hannah visited the pastor to tell him of her concern. She felt that sports-related events could be ideal, since many of the men she had in mind were avid sports fans. Many of them faithfully attended their city's minor league baseball games, and others played golf or went to the local health clubs to play racquetball. Hannah's concern was that these men could be sidetracked in life, so focused on their careers and the pursuit of leisure activities, they gave no thought to their eternal destiny. She felt the church had a responsibility to invest resources in reaching them.

Elisha's servant learned an important lesson as he went out with his master one morning and saw his city surrounded by an enemy army. Not surprisingly he thought the worst, and suspected that his own, Elisha's, and many other lives were in danger. At first, he could not see what Elisha saw; God had sent his own army out in force, and ultimate victory was assured.

In the same way, Hannah cannot see all the resources God has lined up in strategic positions in order to accomplish his will on earth. Quite apart from any investment Hannah's church can make in reaching unbelieving husbands, without a doubt God is working independently, too.

A Suggested Prayer
Thank you, Lord, for the work of your Holy Spirit, your angels, your servants on earth, and for all who invest in your work in our world.

Thank you for bringing me to yourself. Now work in my husband and family too, I pray.

A Question to Answer
Do you, like Elisha, trust God to work in any way he chooses in situations for which you are praying?

Counting the Cost

Will a man rob God? Yet you rob me. MALACHI 3:8

Read: Malachi 3:1-12

Geraldine usually found it a welcome relief to be able to escape from her boisterous but lovable family each Tuesday evening when she attended a small home fellowship group in her neighborhood. There she enjoyed friendship, love, understanding, and support. One day, however, she found herself struggling with a dilemma as they studied the Bible's teachings on giving. She knew that with Chris, her husband, not being a practicing Christian, there was no way she could give much financially to the church. As the study progressed she felt increasingly uneasy.

She listened carefully as the leader explained that God expected the Israelites to give a tithe, meaning a tenth, of their earnings to him, together with additional offerings at other times. She heard that the New Testament principle of giving was based on God's incredible demonstration of love in sending Jesus to our world. Thankfully, the leader was kind and sensitive. He realized that for Geraldine and others this would be a delicate subject, yet he knew it was his task to explain simply and precisely what God's Word says.

It was when the meeting was over and Geraldine stood on the doorstep talking to the leader and his wife that she found peace of mind. They expressed their conviction that women in Geraldine's position cannot give a tenth of the family income because it is not theirs to give. Only if Geraldine's husband agreed could she contribute more than the occasional small gift, but she need not feel guilty. God loves her and completely understands.

Suggested Prayer

I am looking to you for wisdom about this whole delicate area of giving, Lord. Please show me some creative ways that I might give, which will in no way hurt my marriage but will allow me to contribute to the work of your kingdom.

A Practical Suggestion

Today, to show your husband that you love him and care about him, buy something he especially likes, even if it's only his favorite candy bar.

You have kept my word. REVELATION 3:8

Read: Revelation 3:7-13

When Jesus spoke to the church in Philadelphia he identified the huge gulf that exists between those who live according to the ways of the world—and sometimes under the direct influence of Satan—and those who are determined to live for God. Inevitably, when darkness and light are in close proximity, there is tension and conflict, and it is no surprise that Jesus refers to "the hour of trial" (v. 10) his followers have to endure.

Jesus' words are as relevant for us today as for the first-century church. Many Christians struggle against the forces of darkness within their own homes. Janice knew that dreadful pressure. Jack, her husband of over twenty years, thought it was funny when their fourteen-year-old daughter, Chloe, came home drunk from a friend's party. Janice was appalled, both that the parents of Chloe's friend had provided alcohol for these young teenagers, and that Jack had laughed when Chloe staggered home, complaining of how ill she felt. As the sole Christian parent in their home, Janice constantly struggled to maintain God's standards where she could, but that night she felt defeated and afraid for her daughter. How could she teach Chloe the importance of right living when her own husband encouraged irresponsible behavior?

There is no easy answer for Janice. For the time being she is caught between two worlds and two lifestyles. If she were to join Jack and treat Chloe's drunken state merely as a joke, she would know inside she was failing in her duty to God as a Christian parent. On the other hand, if she were critical and judgmental of Chloe, her friend's parents, and Jack, she could find herself alienated from her own family. Janice needs great wisdom from God so she can remain faithful to him while trying to keep relationships intact within the family.

Suggested Prayer

Please help me, Lord, when I feel the tension between the lifestyle you call me to live and to teach my children, and the lifestyles of the world in which I live. Allow my life to be a bright light shining in the darkness.

A Practical Suggestion

When faced with complex situations where you feel you cannot win, do not struggle alone to work out what to do. Meet with a close Christian friend and prayerfully discuss the problem with them. It will probably help a lot.

You have been faithful with a few things. MATTHEW 25:21

Read: Matthew 25:14-30

Hazel had been suspicious for months. Since she and Bob married, he had always taken care of the family's finances. All she did was to glance at the bank statement when it arrived. What first caught her eye was that after years of financial stability, their account was now usually in the red. When she asked Bob about this, he told her prices were rising faster than their income, and there was nothing to worry about.

When Hazel noticed that Bob seemed anxious to intercept the bank statements before she saw them, she began seriously to worry. She knew she had good cause to do so when, having found them, she discovered that for months they had been living on a bank overdraft, although she could not see why their living expenses had risen. As a Christian she believed God would meet the family's needs, a conviction Bob did not share. Hazel believed in using responsibly what God entrusted to them, and she was grateful that her husband, though not a Christian, generally agreed that this was wise.

Hazel finally confronted him, and Bob confessed he had a growing gambling habit. He could not explain why but thought it was to bring back some excitement into his life. After releasing her anger and disappointment, Hazel promised to support Bob in breaking his addiction. They decided to strive together to restore the family's finances to the point where Hazel sensed once again that they were acting as good stewards of what God had given them.

Suggested Prayer
Please give me patience and determination to counteract problems in my life that make me feel uneasy before you, Lord, while also helping me to be sensitive to my husband.

A Question to Answer
Think ... are there any problems relating to your marriage that you are not facing up to at the moment? If so, consider how you can tackle them rather than leaving them unattended and possibly getting worse.

Be holy in all you do. 1 PETER 1:15

Read: 1 Peter 1:13-25

Neither Cheryl nor Jim could understand each other sometimes. Normally they got along well, but there were some occasions when Cheryl wondered why Jim made such bizarre decisions. Similarly, Jim wondered why Cheryl was often so concerned about issues he regarded as relatively unimportant.

Their latest conflict came when Lisa, their teenage daughter, returned home from school one day and asked if she and some friends could attend a play at a theater downtown. Cheryl and Jim not only agreed, but also helped to book the tickets. It seemed like a good opportunity for Lisa to do something special with her friends. Five weeks later, the day before the trip, Cheryl learned from a friend that the play included both nudity and strong language, and she immediately considered it unsuitable for Lisa to see.

Cheryl fully expected Jim's negative response when she told him. Of course, he was exasperated with her for wanting to pull the plug all of a sudden on Lisa's plans. She tried to explain her position: as a Christian, she wanted to eliminate from her own life and the lives of her children those evil influences that corrupt and destroy. Jim, a nominal Christian, argued that Lisa was exposed to those influences at school far more than her mother realized, and that as the evening at the theater had been booked for weeks, Lisa should be allowed to go.

Lisa did go, but Cheryl prayed extra hard for her, expressing to God her regret that she had agreed so quickly to the trip in the first place. God gave her peace, and slowly she began to feel that he at least respected her desire for holiness.

Suggested Prayer

When I get drawn into situations that catch me unaware, please reassure me, Lord, that you understand my dilemma and forgive my naiveté.

A Practical Suggestion

Try to think and plan ahead so you can avert potential problems.

The Power of the Gospel

The Lord opened her heart to respond. ACTS 16:14

Read: Acts 16:11-15

It had been seven years since Julie Ann became a Christian. She had attended a big evangelistic meeting organized by several local churches, heard the gospel for the first time, and was attracted to the positive message of security and reassurance that the preacher had presented. Within two weeks she had made a commitment to Jesus Christ, but because she knew that Frank, her husband, had no religious background, she played down what had happened to her. She went to church most Sundays but never really gave Frank any explanation of the spiritual change that had taken place deep inside her.

Now, seven years later, Frank had stopped worrying about what his wife had gotten into. He had to admit that, if anything, Julie Ann was easier to live with than before, and her friends from church seemed genuine and sincere. Yet he perceived her faith as something that suited her; it never occurred to him that he might benefit from it as well ... until one Christmas Eve when, for the first time, Julie Ann asked Frank to go to church with her. He said he would, and there he heard the same gospel his wife had responded to earlier. It struck a chord in him and within a month he too became a follower of Jesus.

The first question he asked Julie Ann was, "Why didn't you tell me about this before?" Like the presentation of the gospel to Lydia and her household, this one also bore rapid fruit.

Suggested Prayer

Dear Lord, please give me wisdom to know when and how to share the Good News of Jesus with my husband and others close to me who do not yet believe.

A Practical Suggestion

Prepare, both in your mind and in writing, how you will begin and continue a presentation of the gospel to your partner when God gives you opportunities to share it with him.

I have not found such great faith even in Israel. LUKE 7:9

Read: Luke 7:1-10

Times had been troubled for so long for Lynn and Roger that they had agreed to a trial separation, so they could each pursue their separate interests. This meant that at different times each of them agreed to keep the children while the other went out. Even with this arrangement, there was friction over Lynn's numerous activities at her church throughout the week. She tried to be wise as to how many she went to, but Roger frequently told her it was too many.

Now that Roger had been gone from the family home for a couple of months and only called at the house to take the children out, Lynn had time to think and pray. As she reflected, she saw how they had drifted apart, becoming increasingly distant. A crisis of some kind was inevitable. She also recognized that, having become a Christian, there were two important things she had not done. First, she had never really explained her new faith to Roger so that he understood what had happened to her and why she wanted to go to church so often. Second, she had never told him the gospel so that he had a chance to respond to Jesus Christ too.

After asking God to forgive her, Lynn prayed earnestly for Roger in a way she had never done before. She believed that if distance did not prevent Jesus from working in the centurion's servant, nothing need hinder him from working in Roger's life either.

Suggested Prayer
Give me the faith, Lord, to be able to pray for those who are distant from you. Please answer my prayer and work in their lives.

A Question to Answer
Have you imagined your partner becoming a Christian, or someone else close to you who does not yet know the Lord? Pray for this to happen!

71

Partnership with God

The Lord routed Sisera. JUDGES 4:15

Read: Judges 4:4-16

The Israelites achieved a notable victory over Sisera under the leadership of the prophetess Deborah and Barak, the commander of the army. Deborah knew in advance that the Lord had gone ahead of his people and victory was assured. Then it happened as she predicted. Barak and his ten thousand men fought hard, but when victory came, they attributed their success to God. God had promised them the victory, but they also had to work hard—in partnership with God—to accomplish his purposes.

This story held special significance for Josie, because God used it to help redirect her life. She had been uncertain what to do next. She knew that when she and Richard married they had both been thinking about faith, and had spent a lot of time together reading and asking their friends and colleagues what they'd discovered and experienced. Since then Josie had gone one way and become a committed Christian, while Richard had decided not to adhere to any faith but just to remain "open to them all." Josie saw his decision as pure evasion.

This state of affairs had lasted for several years when Josie heard a sermon at church one Sunday that struck her forcibly. The pastor reminded the congregation that God wants to work in the lives of all those people who come within our circle of relationships, especially those who live with us. Using the story of Deborah to illustrate, he explained further that God's way is not to work independently of us, nor to leave us alone to accomplish his work, but for us to work in a remarkable *partnership with him.*

Inspired by this message, Josie committed herself to work in partnership with God instead of trying to wage this battle all alone … or to sit on the sidelines waiting for God to do something. She is confident now that as God works, Richard will become one of his family too. It has changed her entire outlook, and she is fully expectant of the victory God has promised.

Suggested Prayer

Please help me, Lord, to be prepared to let go of my own plans so that I can work in close cooperation with you to see my family and friends brought to faith in Jesus.

A Practical Suggestion

As well as praying for your husband to come to faith in Jesus, talk and pray through with a friend how God can use you best so that he and you cooperate fully together.

The serpent was more crafty. GENESIS 3:1

Read: Genesis 3:1-19

Joan and Paul were exhausted as they entered the counseling center one morning. They had talked and argued for much of the night, and even when they stopped, neither of them had slept. This morning they were due to see their counselor for the fourth time, having been asked to prepare by talking about any interests they had in common. Their discussion had covered the sports and recreational interests that had drawn them together in the first place, and they had debated this fairly amicably. However, it was their respective families, together with Joan's newfound faith, which were the main areas of conflict.

The counselor's nondirective approach was aimed at helping Joan and Paul work out where they thought their relationship was going. She acted simply as a facilitator, but, sadly, as they talked with her, their mood was so negative that neither of them saw much prospect ahead of any stable relationship.

Adam and Eve ate the forbidden fruit in Eden because Satan deceived them both. Today he still likes tricking people into thinking they have freedom to decide whatever they like, irrespective of God's desires. Before deciding the future, Joan especially needs to realize that God has declared marriage to be a permanent uniting of two people. Also, now that she believes in Jesus, Joan's relationship with Paul gives him an opportunity to discover God's love through his Christian wife. If both of them could commit themselves to working at their relationship, and Joan can draw on God's loving resources, there is hope yet!

Prayer Suggestion
When I tend to see our marriage from a purely human perspective, Lord, help me see things from your angle. Then give me hope and a capacity to trust you.

A Question to Answer
Can you think of any reasons why God would not want your marriage to prosper in the future?

God gave knowledge and understanding. DANIEL 1:17

Read: Daniel 1:1-21

Jodie had never traveled far during childhood, and it therefore came as a huge shock when, just four years after she married Tom, his company transferred him to take charge of a department in one of their offices in the Middle East. Jodie's other big surprise in the early days of her marriage was how God called her into a relationship with himself. This was a shock because her family had always frowned on anything to do with religion, but through a neighbor Jodie had heard about Jesus and had responded to his love.

Now Jodie was living in a foreign country surrounded by an unusual culture and a religion she found very hard to understand. She was separated from her family by a huge distance but, like Daniel in Babylon, she found spiritual fellowship in this foreign setting as she met for worship, study, and prayer with other expatriate Christian wives. Together they prayed for husbands like Tom who had not yet come to Christ, and found that God encouraged them through their fellowship.

What thrilled Jodie most was that even here, far from home, God was caring for her and helping her faith to grow. It could have been so different; she could have felt isolated and even given up her faith altogether. She missed her family badly, but being happily married and spending time with her Christian friends, she was able to keep trusting God. As for Tom, she prayed increasingly that he would discover Jesus' love too.

Suggested Prayer
Help me to trust you, Lord, especially if I am away from familiar surroundings, family, and friends. I pray too that my husband will be more open to you away from home.

A Practical Suggestion
Phone or write to someone today who may be far from where you now live, but who you know will support you and your husband in prayer if you ask.

How can I give you up? HOSEA 11:8

Read: Hosea 11:1-11

The eleventh chapter of Hosea is an eloquent reminder that pain is not an alien emotion to the heart of God. He feels great pangs of disappointment and regret when his chosen people, whether Jews or contemporary Christians, go their own way, forget who has sustained them, and put other things or people in his place.

Tiffany was so grateful to know that God understood how she felt. Her sadness was nothing new, but it seemed to hit her harder than usual one weekend. She and Derek had been together for over ten years. Tiffany had only married him after a well-meaning friend had told her what she wanted to hear, that it didn't matter that she was a Christian and Derek was not. If she remained committed to God, she was told, there was nothing to worry about, and Derek would be a believer within a year or two. Tiffany had to learn the hard way that things do not necessarily happen as conveniently as we would like.

Now, some years later, after hearing a sermon at church on the pain God feels, Tiffany was feeling disappointed, yet reassured. She knew that she tended to feel sorry for herself when things didn't go her way, but this was different. Her sadness was caused by her lack of spiritual unity with Derek, and her inability to share her faith with him. Tiffany was reassured that God knew of her pain, and that he too was sad that Derek had not as yet responded to his love.

Suggested Prayer
Heavenly Father, please console me when I need it, and give me the patience and love to be able to handle disappointment.

A Question to Answer
Are you sure you are doing all you can, in cooperation with God, to help what you are praying for to happen?

The body is not meant for sexual immorality. 1 CORINTHIANS 6:13

Read: 1 Corinthians 6:12-20

It happened only rarely, but when an attractive man paid Judy a compliment, it made her knees turn to jelly. It had been like this since she was a teenager and nice-looking boys at school had acted playfully with her. Even now that she was older it had the same effect, despite the fact she was married to Jon and had three children.

It was a casual comment by a man at the office about how nice she looked that began Judy's journey to near disaster. Alan was almost certainly testing her out to see how she responded, but it was hardly any time at all before they began flirting each time they met in the corridor. Then they began to meet after work, telling their respective partners that they were working late. Before long their relationship became adulterous, and while Judy, a Christian for a few years, knew it was thoroughly wrong, the excitement and sense of danger made her block out God's voice completely.

Only several months later did Judy see things differently. Despite the hypocrisy, she had continued to take her children to church, and one Sunday the minister preached about adultery, explaining all the reasons why God calls it sin. For the next few days Judy lived in a confused state, her mind and emotions pulling in different directions. Her eventual desperation drove her to a Christian friend, and after talking and praying, Judy stopped her sinful relationship, rededicated herself to God, and resolved once again to let him use her to help bring her husband to Christ.

Suggested Prayer
Father, please help me see my sin as you see it and understand that if I repent of any sin, you will forgive me.

A Practical Suggestion
Identify three things in your life that you know Jesus would never do, think, or say.

The Spirit of Jesus would not allow them. ACTS 16:7

Read: Acts 16:6-10

While the apostles were pioneer missionaries, God guided them from place to place, often surprising them by closing some doors and opening others. As we see how God used the apostle Paul in Macedonia, it is clear that it was his divine plan for Paul and his friends to go there. Whenever any of us senses God is uneasy about a particular course of action, we need to take time to reassess, pray, and ask him to show us what to do next and when to do it. That's exactly what Pat did when it came to witnessing to her husband, Darrell.

Having believed in Jesus for some years herself, Pat wanted Darrell to come to faith in Jesus too. Soon after her conversion she had decided not to pressure Darrell into coming to church, except on Christmas and Easter. She'd hoped that if she was relaxed about church for the rest of the year, he might choose to accompany her on his own once in a while.

Sadly, however, Darrell had never done so and had even been reluctant to join Pat for seasonal celebrations, especially Easter. One day it dawned on Pat that Darrell was making no headway at all, and that if they were not careful, nothing about this would ever change. This concerned her greatly and made her start praying for some fresh insight and direction from the Lord. Pat needed a new strategy from God as to how to reach Darrell.

Suggested Prayer

Help me to recognize, Lord, any areas of my life that need fresh direction or emphasis. Speak clearly and help me hear your voice.

A Practical Suggestion

Arrange to meet a close Christian friend, or maybe your pastor, to evaluate and pray through your strategy for helping your husband find Jesus Christ personally. Ask God to help you keep an open mind.

Ask for whatever you want me to give you. 2 CHRONICLES 1:7

Read: 2 Chronicles 1:1-12

King Solomon was given one of the greatest privileges of all time when God invited him to ask for anything at all. His choice of "wisdom and knowledge" (v. 10) was essentially not for himself, but so that he could "lead" and "govern" God's people effectively as king. Solomon ensured that his main request to the Lord was for something that would benefit God's work and the lives of others more than himself.

Ann knew her prayers were sometimes too focused on her own needs. You only had to say the word "prayer" in her presence and she would tell you how she was asking God for Phil, her husband, to become a Christian. When an opportunity was given in church or a small group meeting for open prayer, Ann was usually one of the first to participate, and everyone in the church knew the main thing she would ask for from God. They admired her perseverance but felt her prayers were too limited.

One day, one of Ann's friends got up the courage to suggest that there must be other things Ann could pray for. She also inquired why Ann's prayers were preoccupied with Phil. She found out that Ann was so fed up with their fights at home over her Christian faith that she thought her husband's conversion would be the quickest and easiest way to obtain peace. Once Ann recognized that her main motive was selfish, she rethought her prayer strategy and learned to include others in her prayers as well. She kept praying for Phil, although mainly in private, and the church breathed a sigh of relief!

Suggested Prayer
Lord, please help me understand if any of my prayers are essentially selfish. If so, show me ... so that like Solomon I can ask you primarily for things that will benefit others and bring glory to you.

A Practical Suggestion
List each of your prayers today in writing. Then ask God to show you why you prayed for each thing. Were any of your motives selfish?

Expressing Love

How beautiful you are, my darling! SONG OF SOLOMON 4:1

Read: Song of Solomon 4:1-15

Denise was becoming increasingly frustrated by the way her husband, Ken, seemed to take less and less interest in her. Before they were married he was more romantic than any man she had ever met, and he treated her with great respect and courtesy. He often bought her flowers and other gifts, but now, almost three months into their marriage, he was different, and seemed far less romantically inclined. Denise wondered if their relationship was disintegrating, and under the surface she was anxious and frustrated.

The romance expressed by the lovers in the Song of Solomon shows how wholesome and enriching human love can be. This is one of God's gifts to the human race, and this passage describes what Denise thought was the essence of her relationship with Ken. However, what she did not know was that Ken didn't realize there was any change between them, nor did he feel he loved his wife less than before.

This highlights the difference sometimes evident between the sexes. Whereas intimacy and romance are important to women, men are less adept at using words to communicate, especially when it comes to expressions of intimacy. As a newly married man, Ken had unconsciously adopted what he considered to be the role of a husband. He needed gentle encouragement from Denise to see that the romance they had both incorporated into their courtship needed to be an important element in their marriage too.

Suggested Prayer
Dear Lord, please show me how I can best encourage my husband to include romance and intimacy in our relationship if I sense it is missing.

A Practical Suggestion
Make your husband his favorite meal tonight, and serve it in as intimate a setting as you can while trying not to intimidate him or come on too strong.

Nobody should seek his own good, but the good of others.
1 CORINTHIANS 10:24

Read: 1 Corinthians 10:23—11:1

Paul encouraged the Christians in Corinth not to get bound up in unnecessary religious actions, especially if they might hinder other people from discovering God. It is important that everyone has the maximum opportunity to get to know God without Christians hampering them in any way. Indeed, Christians ought to be positive role models who encourage others to follow Jesus too.

Jessica learned the hard way the importance of always guarding what we say and how we act, especially around unbelievers. Her husband, Matt, expressed his extreme disappointment one evening over the behavior of her Christian friends. A group from her church had been to the house for a meeting, and while Matt hadn't been part of it, he had inadvertently heard some of the discussion while he brought in the coffee. He'd been alarmed to hear a barrage of criticism about their pastor, a man whom Matt respected from his occasional encounters with him at a few church events he'd attended. Matt felt let down to hear Christians speaking like this of their leader; not only did it concern him, it also disillusioned him. He thought Christianity had a strong emphasis on love and care and actively discouraged critical attitudes. He was right, of course.

Jessica was acutely embarrassed when Matt explained his reaction. She apologized, although she knew that much damage had already been done, and she promised to tell her friends so that this would never happen again.

Suggested Prayer
Help me to be sensitive to other people, Lord, and never hinder others from finding you. As far as possible, please protect my husband from anything that will stop him from encountering your love.

A Practical Suggestion
Whenever you speak with other people today, try to think through how they may be responding to what you say. Are they hearing Christian attitudes?

Being Part of the Family

*My mother and brothers are those who hear God's word
and put it into practice.* LUKE 8:21

Read: Luke 8:19-21

Compared to some of her other friends whose husbands did not share their faith, Erin knew she had it easy. Jeremy was more cooperative than many Christian husbands when it came to helping and encouraging her in her faith. He would try to get home from work early if she asked him to so that she could attend church events, and on Sundays he would prepare lunch while the family went to church. Nor did Jeremy have any problem with the children saying grace before meals or Erin reading Bible stories to them at bedtime. The only dilemma for Erin was that while Jeremy was wonderfully supportive of her faith, he had none of his own, nor did he seem to be seeking it.

When Jesus was told that his relatives had come to see him, he explained that his family are those who not only know God's truth but apply it in their lives. Erin was familiar with this Scripture, and it concerned her that, while Jeremy agreed with the essence of Christian teaching, he'd made no personal commitment to accept it for himself. The saddest thing for Erin was that Jeremy was so near to God's kingdom, yet so far away.

People like Jeremy often see no need to change, because their life is fairly comfortable. Their position is akin to sitting on a fence, and something has to happen before they are ever seriously likely to reevaluate their life. In this situation, Erin needs to keep praying.

Suggested Prayer
Father, where I know someone who needs fresh insight into spiritual things, show me how best to pray for them and serve them. Please draw them into your family.

A Question to Answer
Have you resolved to live as closely as you can to the teaching of God's Word in every area of your life?

Explaining Your Position

Always be prepared to give an answer. 1 PETER 3:15

Read: 1 Peter 3:8-22

Evenings were often traumatic times in Georgie and Malcolm's home, and the TV and VCR were usually at the center of their disagreements. Their fifteen-year-old son Andy wanted to watch the same programs and movies as his dad, but if Georgie was uneasy about her husband watching gratuitous sex and violence, she was thoroughly opposed to Andy seeing them. However, Malcolm had no problem with it, believing that Andy needed exposure to the "real" world.

One evening, Malcolm arrived home from work with a stack of R-rated videos. When Georgie protested, Malcolm threw up his hands in disgust. "I've had it with this, Georgie. It's time you let the kid grow up!" He then spoke with disdain of Georgie and her church friends who seemed, in his view, to "have their heads stuck in the sand," trying to live in a whitewashed world that didn't exist.

Georgie gave up her struggle that evening and let Andy watch the movies with his father. There really was no way she could stop it. All she could do (and often she felt guilty because she thought it was inadequate) was to watch along with them and try to talk to Andy afterward about what he saw, explaining simply and honestly how she felt about it and why.

Being ready to explain why is important for every believer. It applies to every situation—whether faced with unbelievers who challenge Christian beliefs, or simply being asked why you've made certain choices. On the whole, others will show at least some respect for those whose choices are different than their own, if they can explain the principles behind them. Georgie's prayer is that as she tries to do this, both Andy and Malcolm will hear what she says and be affected positively by it. And she prays diligently that Andy will not mimic his father's negative attitudes, but will come to see the wisdom of a Christ-centered life.

Suggested Prayer

Help me, Lord, to think clearly and express my faith succinctly when there are opportunities to do so. When I share with my husband, help him to listen and understand.

A Practical Suggestion

If people you live with misunderstand any part of your Christian faith, try to work out why. Then, when the time is right, explain your position to them.

An offended brother is more unyielding than a fortified city.
PROVERBS 18:19

Read: Proverbs 18:1-20

Jason and Melissa were genuinely concerned that their seventeen-year-old son, Jerry, was heading for trouble. He was rude, offensive, and uncommunicative, and he irritated his mother in particular by treating his home like a hotel and expecting everyone to clean up after him. He also spent much of his time with a group of friends who seemed even more rough and uncouth than he was. Jason and Melissa sensed that at any time Jerry could get into trouble with the law, and even face the prospect of a prison sentence.

As they talked about their fears, they began to realize that they may have contributed to the negative attitude Jerry now had toward them. Jerry had grown up listening to his parents bicker and argued—often about Melissa's faith. She had become a Christian when Jerry was born prematurely and was not expected to live long. It was only skilled nursing and prayer that ensured his survival. In her distress, Melissa had turned to God. He became so real to her that from then on her life centered on God. Jason resented this, and Jerry grew up among frequent arguments, mainly about when his mother could and could not go to church.

As they saw that their parenting had been deficient and Jerry was probably rebelling against the atmosphere in which he'd grown up, Jason and Melissa agreed to talk with Jerry together and ask for their son's forgiveness. They sensed it could do no harm, and might help to repair the broken relationships.

Suggested Prayer

Dear Lord, please help my husband and me to see clearly any mistakes we've made in our parenting that may be rebounding on us today. Then give us the grace and humility to apologize if that seems appropriate.

A Practical Suggestion

Think back to specific days and events you recall spending with your children, maybe together as a family. Relive one or two in your imagination, and evaluate what it must have been like to have you and your husband as parents.

A Constant Supply

The jug of oil did not run dry. 1 KINGS 17:16

Read: 1 Kings 17:7-24

Lillian had had a tough time at home for many years. She and Dave, her husband, certainly loved each other, but he really could not understand why she had become a Christian several years earlier. He did not appreciate all the phone calls from her church friends whom he did not know, nor was he too excited about a weekly prayer group that met in their home one lunchtime each week. He felt excluded from an area of Lillian's life that she obviously enjoyed, and sometimes his frustration and disappointment came to the surface.

Lillian found that she coped best with the tension at home by praying more and taking extra time to share her feelings openly and honestly with God. She couldn't explain how it happened, but as she talked to God he somehow strengthened and encouraged her, enabling her to carry on. In Elijah's day too, God proved his love and faithfulness to a woman and her family by miraculously supplying resources that they desperately needed.

God's remarkable capacity of knowing precisely what our needs are, and then being able to meet them, is highly reassuring as we face up to each day's tensions and problems. As the apostle Paul found, God does not always remove those things with which we struggle; rather he gives us special grace and power to rise above them (2 Cor 12:7-10). Lillian's experience is that God has never let her down, even though sometimes life at home is not easy.

Suggested Prayer

Dear Lord, help me to trust you, especially when things at home are demanding and I feel out of my depth. Please stand close beside me, and pour out your grace and strength into my life.

A Practical Suggestion

Read through the Gospels and count how many times Jesus came to the rescue of his disciples when they were struggling and getting out of their depth.

Just say whatever is given you at the time. MARK 13:11

Read: Mark 13:1-13

Janine was fuming by the time she arrived home with her husband, Robert, from a dinner party at a friend's house. She had expected to enjoy a quiet and relaxed evening with their friends. However, during the meal Robert began to make fun of the fact that Janine had recently started attending church, and their friends soon joined in. In fact, all three of them turned on Janine, who felt both overwhelmed and threatened by the rather harsh and intimidating questions they posed. Having been a Christian for only a few weeks, she struggled with some of her answers, and she felt she let the Lord down by her hesitant replies. When they got back home, Janine told Robert how angry she was with him for having started this off.

While training his disciples, Jesus prepared them as fully as possible for the persecution they would face by remaining loyal to him. Physical punishment and judicial proceedings would be among the painful experiences they would have to endure. Later, of course, he himself had to cope with all of this—and more—as he suffered for the sins of the world.

Although Janine's experience did not take place in a courtroom, she was certainly interrogated about her faith by those who intended to make her look foolish. Yet God was with her through this ordeal, as he promises to be when his children are put on the spot for their faith. Indeed, Robert had found Janine's simple but honest answers full of such conviction that he quickly apologized when they were at home and promised never to do this to her again.

Suggested Prayer
Please be close to me, Lord, and guide me whenever I am called to give account of my faith. Give me the ability to trust you in these demanding times.

A Practical Suggestion
Start keeping a notebook of comments about "Why I Believe." Challenge yourself with some questions about the Christian faith and write down your answers. Let this be a tool to help you think through your faith clearly, but remember also that God tells us in his Word not to *worry* about what we will say when put on trial for our faith. When that happens, we can trust the Holy Spirit to give us the right words.

Accept one another, then, just as Christ accepted you.
ROMANS 15:7

Read: Romans 15:1-13

Janey was unbelievably ecstatic when, after several weeks of encouraging her husband to go with her to her church's carol service, he agreed. This was her first Christmas as a Christian, and she had been looking for opportunities to invite Mike to an event where the gospel would be explained. She was so eager for them to be united in the Christian faith, she prayed hard that once Mike got there, he would enjoy it and understand the truth of the gospel.

What happened after the service and over the next couple of weeks, however, turned Janey's ecstasy to pain. She was disappointed after the carol service because hardly anyone from the church greeted Mike or talked to him. Then whenever she went to church over the next few weeks, she was met with a barrage of questions, mainly inquiring whether Mike had become a Christian at Christmas. She sensed that no one was very interested in Mike as a person, and Janey became increasingly uneasy about inviting him back to church. She felt this insensitive attitude would come across to Mike and only hinder his progress toward the kingdom of God.

Soon afterward, Janey decided to tell her minister of her disappointment. He listened sympathetically and, while agreeing to her request for confidentiality, said he would talk with the congregation about the need to be sensitive and to support lone Christian wives more in various ways. He agreed that the church must not make it more difficult for these wives to encourage their husbands to become Christians.

Prayer Suggestion
Please use me in any way you can, Lord, to show others in my church the kind of support and encouragement I and other lone Christian wives need.

A Question to Answer
Have you given any support and encouragement recently to another Christian wife whose husband is not a believer?

Expressing Devotion

Mary took about a pint of pure nard ... she poured it on Jesus' feet.
JOHN 12:3

Read: John 12:1-8

Before she became a Christian, Mariah had had an affair with a neighbor, a choice that affected her husband very deeply. After that he found it very difficult to trust his wife with other men, and easily became suspicious and jealous because he expected the worst. Initially, he did not see any problem when Mariah told him she had become a Christian, but as time went on he grew jealous of the extreme importance her faith had in her life. Alarm bells started to ring, and he tried to discourage her from attending church so often.

For Mariah, committing her life to Jesus was a wonderful experience. She loved him very much because of all he had done for her, especially the forgiveness he had freely given to her for her past indiscretion. In no time at all Mariah's friends knew what had happened to her. Her newfound faith bubbled from within her and she was a radiant witness for Jesus.

Jesus never complains when his friends express their love and commitment to him. Having said that, it is not a complete surprise, given the circumstances, that Mariah's husband finds any man a threat—even Jesus! This couple probably needs counseling to help work through and resolve this painful past episode. Then, and only then, will Mariah find she can express her passion for Jesus without fear of her husband misunderstanding.

Suggested Prayer
Heavenly Father, please give my husband and me courage to work through any past hurts that threaten to disrupt our lives now and in the future.

A Question to Answer

How many past hurts and grievances are still alive and lurking in rarely opened cupboards of your marriage, ready to pounce out when you least expect them? If you discern any, try to resolve them with your husband now, before any past problem becomes an explosive issue.

Standing Out from the Crowd

It is God's will that you should be holy. 1 THESSALONIANS 4:3

Read: 1 Thessalonians 4:1-12

Jessica had always known that her husband, Brian, could be pretty vulgar. She saw traces of it at home sometimes, but it was primarily when he was with his friends at the bar that it was most obvious. Jessica had always tried not to go with him, but lately, since becoming a Christian, she resisted his pressure more fiercely than ever. She had always felt embarrassed by his behavior at bars, but now she found that what he said, and the way he said it, was both crude and offensive. Whenever she went with him now, she kept very quiet and spent her time silently asking God to forgive her and strengthen her.

In many of the letters in the New Testament there is strong encouragement to live a holy lifestyle that makes God's children stand out from the crowd. Jessica knew this and, secretly, she envied her female Christian friends whose husbands also had a personal faith. She felt they were highly unlikely to have to cope with the kind of pressure she was under. Jessica's dream was that was one day Brian would have a Damascus Road experience of Jesus, and that overnight he would become totally reformed.

In the meantime Jessica has to look to God for his strength, because she has a delicate balancing act to do. While God still calls her to live a holy life, she knows she must not alienate Brian or destroy the relationship they have. After all, she married him "for better, for worse," and now, as she keeps praying for him, she must give him her support, but without compromising herself before God.

Suggested Prayer

Please be especially close to me, Lord, when I find myself pulled in different directions. I am so glad you understand the pressure I am under. Help me to love and support my husband despite this.

A Practical Suggestion

If your husband likes to go out to drink, try to find a place you can visit together sometimes where you feel comfortable.

Not seven times, but seventy-seven times. MATTHEW 18:22

Read: Matthew 18:21-35

Only after she married him did Camille discover what she considered to be a perverse tendency in Ryan. For some unknown reason he seemed to relish people making mistakes. Invariably, he responded by mocking them, although rarely to their faces, but he had no reservation about doing so to Camille. When she became a Christian his expectations for her rose, and consequently she had to tolerate his mocking on a regular basis at home. She didn't find it easy to cope with this but tried to be patient.

However, things deteriorated when Camille's church ran into trouble over a controversy that split the congregation in half. Unfortunately, Ryan worked with the husband of another woman who attended the church, and he found out about it. He also discovered that this man's wife and Camille had opposing points of view, which made the situation at home more difficult for Camille. Ryan came home some nights appearing to relish the fact that he knew more sordid details of the church's bitter split, and he taunted Camille with what he knew until she began to dread his return from work.

Camille discussed the problem with one of her close friends, who strongly advised her not to get drawn into discussions about the church. She also encouraged Camille to ask God constantly for the capacity to forgive Ryan. Harboring resentment and bitterness would only hamper her own spiritual growth and relationship with the Lord.

Suggested Prayer
Lord, as you relentlessly forgive me when I ask you, please give me the same capacity to forgive my husband or anyone else who makes my life more difficult.

A Question to Answer
When did you last meditate on all that Jesus went through to secure forgiveness for you? Try it!

A Big Turnaround

God changed Saul's heart. 1 SAMUEL 10:9

Read: 1 Samuel 10:1-16

When we become open to what God can do for us, God will start to work miracles. Saul made himself available for God's will to be done in his life as he listened to Samuel's prophetic words, and God changed him from the inside.

Sophie was well aware of what God had done for her, especially the miracles he had worked within her. Only two years earlier she had been drinking heavily and finding it hard to hold her life together. She was making steady progress in her career, but the increasing pressure on her to perform ever more successfully was taking its toll. The lunchtime drinks sustained her during the afternoon, while most evenings were spent in a bar. Mercifully for her marriage, her husband liked to drink too.

One day the stark reality of Sophie's situation hit her and she turned to a friend for help. Katherine was the wife of the pastor of a nearby church, and she willingly worked with Sophie. As they talked, Katherine told Sophie about God's love and the opportunity for a relationship with him through faith in Jesus Christ. After many months of searching, Sophie gave her life to Jesus. She stopped drinking excessively and, with Katherine's encouragement and support, began to grow spiritually.

Sophie's main concern now is for Graham, her husband, who has noticed the change in her, but so far has resisted the opportunity to discover more about God for himself. Sophie knows now how much God is willing and able to change us, and she looks for any hopeful signs that Graham is becoming more open to God. She continues to pray for Graham, believing God for her next big miracle!

Suggested Prayer

I praise you, Lord, that you can and do work deeply in people's lives to change them. Thank you for what you have done for me. Work in those close to me, and help me to pray faithfully until they respond.

A Practical Suggestion

In order to encourage your faith in God to grow, read a Christian book that illustrates God's life-changing power.

I also want women to dress modestly. 1 TIMOTHY 2:9

Read: 1 Timothy 2:8-15

God does not have a problem with Christians looking attractive. When Timothy received his letter, prostitutes were commonplace in Ephesus, and Paul saw the importance of Christian women being visibly different as a witness to God. He wasn't asking women to make themselves dowdy in order to appear modest; he simply wanted them not to look like prostitutes! As modern-day Christians, we need to wisely interpret such practical biblical instruction in light of our own culture, and what is considered appropriate or modest now.

George is a man who was turned off to Christianity at an early age because of the many strict rules he had to live under while growing up—rules he thought God had unfairly imposed on people who believed in him. He had had a thorough grounding in the stories and teaching of the Bible, but as a teenager, he rejected both Christianity and the church. Then he later met and married Linda, whose background was completely godless. It came as a surprise to George when, after a decade together, Linda told him she was going to a special meeting at a nearby church where a famous Christian sportsman was speaking. He was even more shocked when she came home with the announcement that she had become a Christian.

It was then that their problems began. George's strict Christian upbringing made him fearful that Linda would now be changed in ways he wasn't willing to accept. George's Christian mother and aunt had always dressed in dull colors and refused to wear makeup and jewelry, on principle. His mother had explained to him that, according to Paul's letter to Timothy, women would dishonor God if they dressed in a way that drew attention to themselves. George had always struggled with this, but was now anxious that his own attractive wife would rethink her image.

Following a hasty talk with some new Christian friends, Linda reassured George that, while she had changed inside by trusting in Jesus

Christ, she was not about to throw out her wardrobe, jewelry, and makeup. She agreed with him that his mother and aunt had probably gone overboard in their understanding of Paul's instruction to the first-century church. She certainly didn't believe that God expected her to dress unattractively now, and she put George at ease over the whole issue.

Suggested Prayer

Lord, please give me wisdom when deciding what clothes and accessories to wear. I want everything about me to help other people to see you.

A Practical Suggestion

Take another look through your closet in case you have anything that you now feel, as a Christian, would be inappropriate to wear.

Parenting Pain

Train a child in the way he should go. PROVERBS 22:6

Read: Proverbs 22:1-9

Although a lone spiritual parent because her husband was not a Christian, Sherry was committed to raising her children to follow Jesus Christ. Ever since they were babies, she had taken them to church, prayed for them, and told them Bible stories at home. She believed it was important to give them a thorough spiritual training, and her only regret was that her husband completely distanced himself from this.

Everything ran smoothly until Sherry's eldest son, Joey, was nine. By then he had noticed that his father never went to church and seemed to do much more interesting things at home while the rest of the family was at worship. One day Joey asked his dad if he could stay home with him on Sundays instead of going to church, and hearing that he could, informed his mom of his intentions. The bitter argument between Joey's parents over this decision was one he did not forget.

Sherry gently confronted her husband for making it too easy for Joey to break what for him was the habit of a lifetime. She also prayed intently while reminding Joey of his many friends at church, and of the collection of prizes he had won, to which he could add if he came back. Eventually, a few months later, after some of his friends had pestered him to return, Joey was back at church on Sunday mornings. Sherry breathed a sigh of relief and said a sincere prayer of thanks to God.

Suggested Prayer

Father, please help me as a Christian parent to give strong yet sensitive direction to my children, so that they learn about you naturally in their formative years.

A Question to Answer

Is there anything else that God wants you to do to help your children learn about God and his love while they are young?

My lover is mine and I am his. SONG OF SOLOMON 2:16

Read: Song of Solomon 2:1-17

The news that her best friend's marriage was on the verge of collapse brought Sara up with a start. She had always presumed that Ruth's relationship with Arnold was strong and happy, but now she'd learned that her friends felt they had very little in common anymore and were going to separate on a trial basis. This made Sara think. When she and Larry married they pursued all kinds of sporting and outdoor activities together, but now, with her becoming a mother and a Christian, and Larry getting a promotion at work, they rarely spent much time alone together relaxing. She decided to do something about it.

Sara looked at her engagement calendar and found the next evening both she and Larry would be free. She asked him to reserve it for a surprise occasion. She decided she would put the children to bed early, serve Larry's favorite meal by candlelight, and ask him to read a selection of the love letters he'd written to her while they were dating.

After their romantic dinner, Sara was amazed at the impact of such a simple occasion. The distance that had built up between them vanished, including, it seemed, Larry's uneasiness about Sara becoming a Christian. As they laughed and cuddled on the sofa they felt young and carefree again, and Sara thanked God for inspiring her to do something that was so beneficial to their relationship.

Suggested Prayer
Dear Lord, help me to listen to you and to think creatively about ways in which I can rejuvenate my marriage.

A Practical Suggestion
Create your own special evening with your husband. Above all, make it fun!

93 *Listening to God*

After the fire came a gentle whisper. 1 KINGS 19:12

Read: 1 Kings 19:1-18

Danelle was never clear why Peter's attitude toward her had changed. It was not because she'd become a Christian, since she already was one, albeit backslidden, when they married. However, a few months back she had recommitted her life to Christ, and God became substantially more important to her than ever before. Maybe Peter was uncomfortable with her greater desire now to pray and live a holy life.

The main change in Peter's behavior was the way he began to swear and use language that Danelle found seriously offensive. At first she reacted strongly, ordering him to stop, but he seemed to enjoy upsetting her and deliberately continued. Danelle didn't know what to do, but over a period of weeks, she discovered that by not responding to his anger and bad language, he stopped sooner than if she objected.

Danelle's biggest problem at this point became her sense of guilt and shame before God over the blasphemous language that filled her home. Initially, this hindered her relationship with God, but a good Christian friend reminded her that at times like this she needed God more than ever. Danelle committed herself to spending a little longer each day in Bible study and prayer. If ever there was a time when she needed to hear the reassuring whisper of God's voice, this was it.

Suggested Prayer
Please reassure and help me, Lord, when I find myself deeply troubled by the behavior of others around me. Let me know that you understand and will support me.

A Question to Answer
Did you notice in today's Bible reading how God recommissioned Elijah, and told him to go back to continue the kind of work he was doing before?

Feeling the Loss

Jesus wept. JOHN 11:35

Read: John 11:1-44

Joshua was hurting, but Miranda could not work out what the problem was. She kept on asking him why he had lost his usual enjoyment of life and seemed to be permanently sad. When he would not tell her, she spoke to her pastor's wife, but even after talking and praying about it, they could not speculate as to the cause. Joshua's job was secure, and nothing in his life had changed. To Miranda, her husband's change of demeanor was a mystery.

However, under the surface, Joshua was struggling to cope with what Miranda had told him a few weeks before. She had shared with him how much she loved Jesus Christ, who was now her best friend, but she was completely unaware of Joshua's response. He now felt pushed out and excluded within his own marriage. He was devastated that his loving wife of twelve years, and whose integrity he did not doubt for a moment, now had another man occupying her thoughts. He was grieving because he felt he had lost her, and yet she still lived in the same house and they shared the same bed.

When Jesus' friend Lazarus died, he was deeply sad. This is the normal human reaction when anyone we love is wrenched from us. Miranda and other wives in her situation must be careful not to unsettle their husbands with their newfound relationship with Jesus. Husbands, of course, are not at risk when their wives love Jesus too, but they may feel they have somehow lost their love.

Suggested Prayer

Help me, Lord, to be gentle and sensitive in how I witness to those who are close to me.

A Question to Answer

Have you ever planned how you will share your faith with your husband when a spontaneous opportunity arises? Do it!

They may be won over without talk. 1 PETER 3:1

Read: 1 Peter 3:1-7

Elaine and Tony's wedding attracted the attention of the local newspaper reporters and a TV crew. This young couple had grown up in the same neighborhood, played together as preschoolers, and attended the same schools from kindergarten through high school. They were good friends in elementary school, and started dating in their teens. Their friendship and love for each other deepened over the years. They even attended the local community college together rather than go their separate ways. After graduating, they decided to marry. The media became interested over this "Hometown Boy Marries Childhood Sweetheart" story—not a very frequent occurrence these days with so many families on the move.

After a couple of years of marriage, Elaine found herself working with a young woman who was a committed Christian. Her attitude toward life and her job, together with her genuine warmth and care for others, attracted Elaine to build a friendship with her. Within a few months Elaine had heard the Good News, and only a few weeks later she made a personal commitment of her life to Jesus Christ.

God worked deeply in her life from the outset, and soon Elaine was asking her friend how she could best help Tony to become a Christian too. It did not take long before Elaine realized the best way. At home, she would simply be herself and live as someone whose life had been changed by Jesus. She did not need to preach or be pushy. Tony had known her for so long that he could hardly fail to notice how much she had changed—from the inside out!

Suggested Prayer

Heavenly Father, please help me to be a strong, vibrant witness in front of my family, who have known me for so long. Help them to see how much you have changed my life.

A Practical Suggestion

See if you can find some other Christian wives in similar circumstances to yours. Then share and pray together about the way you can witness at home.

> *Whenever ... the rainbow appears in the clouds,*
> *I will remember my covenant.* GENESIS 9:14-15

Read: Genesis 9:1-17

Louise felt generally disheartened. She was not happy in her job, her best friend had just moved away, and she felt isolated at church, largely because most of the married couples her age worshiped together with their spouses. Louise always felt conspicuous walking into church alone. She prayed regularly for Nick's conversion, but so far he had not responded at all. Overall, life was hard going and she could not see what might change to make it any easier.

Having been in church circles for years, Louise knew that Christians sometimes suffer crises of faith, although she never had herself. That was until she found a number of problems start to pile up and overwhelm her. A troubling thought kept flooding her mind, even though she tried to push it away: "Where is God in all this?" she asked, as she struggled to work out how she felt and why.

One evening as she looked out of her living room window, God spoke to her without saying a word. After a day of torrential rains and lightning storms, the clouds had broken and a magnificent rainbow stretched across the darkening sky. Louise could not help but remember God's promise to Noah. As she reflected on the fact that God would be faithful whatever happened, she found her heart being warmed and her spirit coming alive. In that moment she knew God had not abandoned her—and never would!

Suggested Prayer
I want to thank you, Lord, for your faithfulness to me so far, and also for your promise that whatever happens in the future you will never leave me nor forsake me.

A Question to Answer
Apart from the rainbow, what other signs has God shown you that have expressed his faithfulness to you?

Unless I see the nail marks in his hands… JOHN 20:25

Read: John 20:19-31

It was only after becoming a Christian that Marie realized how fitting it was that her husband's name was Tom. When Marie first heard the Christian gospel she took time to reflect on her life and what Jesus had to offer, but within three months she had come to the point where she was ready to commit her life to him. Immediately she entered into a relationship with Jesus that she found both real and meaningful.

Marie wasted no time in telling Tom about this, but he was skeptical from the start. As a scientist, he was not prepared to "hope" that the Bible was true. He reasoned that unless it can be proved that God exists, that Jesus is his Son, and that Jesus' death and resurrection actually happened and have some kind of bearing on people today, he would dismiss it as yet another fairy tale.

Reading the Bible, Marie saw that Tom's namesake, the disciple Thomas, had problems believing in Jesus too. Despite being told of Jesus' appearance among his friends by people he would normally have trusted, Thomas could not accept that he had risen from the dead. Only when he met Jesus and saw his wounds did Thomas accept it as the truth. Marie knew that Tom would not have the privilege of an encounter like that, so she committed herself to pray that God would find another way to break through to him to bring him to faith.

Suggested Prayer
Dear Lord, please help my husband learn to place his trust and faith in you. Let him recognize the reality of your new life in me.

A Question to Answer
If you were accused in a court of law of being a Christian, what evidence could be presented to support the claim?

The Pain of Discipleship

All men will hate you because of me. MATTHEW 10:22

Read: Matthew 10:1-23

From the time her children were very young, Vicki believed in the importance of reading them stories, and had accumulated a substantial pile of books by the time her fourth child was old enough to appreciate them. The *Cat in the Hat* books were some of three-year-old Janette's favorites, and she asked for them every night at bedtime. Just before Janette was born, Vicki had become a Christian and began reading the Bible seriously for herself. In it she discovered some remarkable and dramatic stories, and it dawned on her that Janette and her older brothers would enjoy them too. Having bought a children's Bible, she started to read to them before they went to bed and they were often enthralled by what they heard.

Philip, Vicki's husband, was far from sure that this was a good idea, and wasted no time in telling her so. He had grown up in a family that was very skeptical about anything religious, and he was adamant that he didn't want his children indoctrinated or brainwashed. Sadly, Vicki and Philip violently disagreed about this issue many times, with neither being prepared to back down. Vicki kept reading the Bible to the children each night while Philip threatened to tear up the book and throw it away.

Jesus knew that throughout future generations people would disagree about matters of faith, and at times families would be torn apart because someone trusted in him. This does not make life any easier for Vicki, but at least she knows she is not alone in paying a high price for following Jesus.

Suggested Prayer
Having experienced the wonder of your love to me personally, Lord, I ask for your strength to persevere when it is not easy to remain faithful to you.

A Practical Suggestion
Reflect on the cost Jesus paid for your forgiveness and salvation.

Responding to God's Love

Each one of you should set aside a sum of money. 1 CORINTHIANS 16:2

Read: 1 Corinthians 16:1-9

The sermon Paula heard in church one Sunday took her by surprise. One of the reasons she had selected this particular church when she became a Christian was that it seemed to make very little reference to money. Earlier in life, Paula had attended Sunday school in a church that seemed preoccupied by its lack of money. They were always holding yard sales, and even erected a huge wooden sign painted with a red thermometer to show the whole community how impoverished they were.

Paula had no doubt that the sermon her pastor preached was good and true, but it left her with a problem. She was the only Christian at home, and Terry, her husband, had only limited sympathy for her church and faith. Furthermore, he controlled the family finances, and all their money went into a joint account. What was she to do now that she had heard the pastor preach that sacrificial and proportionate giving were encouraged in the Bible? How could she possibly find more money than the dollar or two she took from the loose change in her purse each week?

As she discussed her dilemma with a friend, Paula felt she was in a no-win situation. Terry was unlikely to agree to her giving anything much to church, and it would be dishonest to withdraw money from their joint account for such a purpose without his knowing. Yet as things stood, she felt guilty before God, so she decided to pray about it until his solution became clear.

Suggested Prayer
Father, please give me your clear guidance over the issue of money. How can I give to your work, Lord, and still keep harmony at home?

A Practical Suggestion
If your husband has complete control of your finances, consider talking with him about how any money you earn is used in your overall budget. Would it be fair and reasonable for you to allocate some of it to a church, ministry, or charity of your choice?

Make every effort to live in peace. HEBREWS 12:14

Read: Hebrews 12:14-29

Neither Jason nor Naomi could work out what was the matter with Julia, their seventeen-year-old daughter. They managed one day to have a civilized discussion about her—a rare occurrence, since Jason had become irritable and hard to talk with following Naomi's conversion to Christianity. He had always valued their weekends together and was none too pleased when she began going to church most Sundays.

For the past few months Julia had been noticeably uncommunicative at home. She told her parents virtually nothing about her studies, her feelings, or her plans. They managed to extract snippets of information from her occasionally, but their once warm, friendly, and outgoing daughter had become ill-tempered, moody, and introspective—with them at least. Jason and Naomi were increasingly worried about her, in case she was being drawn into anything sinister that she didn't want them to find out about.

Thankfully, Julia attended the church youth group, so her parents agreed that Naomi would talk discreetly to the pastor, whose home Julia often visited because she was friends with his daughter. Martin, the pastor, was reluctant to say much, but revealed that he'd heard how upset Julia was that her parents often had disagreements at home. He said she had consciously decided not to take sides, and felt that her best form of protection was to distance herself from both parents for the time being. The challenge to Jason and Naomi was to resolve their own problem before it had a long-term effect on Julia.

Suggested Prayer

Lord, I am actively committed to working out any unhappy personal relationships that are having a negative and destructive effect on my family. Please help me.

A Practical Suggestion

If you are in a relationship that has gone sour, determine that you will work to put it right whatever it costs and however long it takes.

When you pass through the waters, I will be with you. ISAIAH 43:2

Read: Isaiah 43:1-7

Everyone has to cope with tough periods in life, but for Brenda it had lasted long enough. Her most obvious difficulty was coming to terms with her mother's death. They had always been very close, but when her mom was diagnosed as terminally ill, Brenda's life began to collapse. While she had left home two decades before, she had begun to lean on her mother for support when her own marriage began feeling cool. Her mother had been a loving and gracious source of comfort, never telling her daughter what to do but simply being in the background if she needed to talk or cry.

Her mother's death left a big gap in Brenda's life. Sadly, it came at a time when her son's health was worrying her too. Tim was fourteen and experiencing pain in his abdomen that had his doctor baffled. He had been referred to a specialist, but the appointment had not arrived by the time Brenda's mother passed away. At the funeral, Brenda felt isolated and drained. Her husband, although present, seemed emotionally distant. They both knew he had never come to terms with the commitment to Jesus Christ she had made some seven years before. She appreciated his being there, but she still felt alone.

The minister who conducted the funeral service read Isaiah 43 before giving his meditation. Brenda found the words wonderfully reassuring and sensed that God was reminding her of his personal care. While her pain and problems remained, Brenda went home knowing God was with her and that she was safe.

Suggested Prayer
Dear Lord, when I feel alone, please come and reassure me of your love and support. Let me know you will be with me whatever happens.

A Practical Suggestion
Read a Christian biography that tells how another believer has discovered God's help and strength in demanding times.

Using God's Gifts Wisely

Jonathan had David reaffirm his oath out of love for him.
1 SAMUEL 20:17

Read: 1 Samuel 20:1-23

Although they had never discussed it, both Lois and Brad knew their relationship was not close. Their wedding had been a mere fourteen weeks after they first met, and they both knew that had they waited, they probably would have never married at all. Now, not wanting to hurt each other, they had settled into a pattern of life that provided each of them with comparative freedom.

Lois began to feel uncomfortable about her marriage a few months after reading a gospel tract she'd found on the commuter train on her way to work. Knowing that Christians go to church, she decided to visit one near their apartment and, enjoying it, began to go regularly. She soon struck up a friendship with Jo, a young woman about her age. Their relationship grew as Jo encouraged Lois to follow Jesus and devote herself to serving him. Lois was extremely happy to be a Christian and to have solid friendships with Jo and the other Christians she was meeting.

Deep and loving friendships are part of God's gift to us. David and Jonathan were both blessed by the care and support of the other at a demanding time in their lives. Lois too felt blessed by her new friendships; however, she began to see that she also needed wisdom where her marriage was concerned. If her relationship with Brad was shaky before she'd become a Christian, then he could easily be edged out of her life completely now that God and her new Christian friends were so important to her. Lois knew she needed God's help to try to rebuild her marriage before it was too late.

Suggested Prayer

Lord, please motivate me to work at any important relationships in my life with insecure foundations.

A Practical Suggestion

Evaluate, in a brutally honest way, the most important relationships in your life. Work out which three are most important, and consider before God whether or not this order is acceptable.

Who will go for us? ISAIAH 6:8

Read: Isaiah 6:1-10

Ten years ago Maggie became a Christian, but she knew only too well that she hadn't made much headway since. While to some extent she was able to play the part at church, she was aware that the attitudes her family saw at home were not very spiritual. She longed to become a more genuine Christian, but didn't know how it could happen.

Then one Sunday night at church something took Maggie by surprise. Her pastor had just returned from visiting a church that had been spiritually renewed, and somehow he seemed to bring God's presence into the worship. Maggie could not easily find words to describe what happened that evening, but she found herself responding to God in a deeper way than ever before. Suddenly she became aware of Jesus' rich love for her and it moved her deeply. She burst into tears, not so much from sadness—although she did repent of her past apathy—but from relief that Jesus had come to her and was now ministering to her hurts and disappointment.

Even after leaving the service, Maggie could still feel God's presence strongly. Then she found herself thinking of her husband and sensed God prompting her to tell him the gospel. It was a divine call to a specific task. In the same way Isaiah had an encounter with God, so Maggie was being challenged by God to commit herself to serving him in a new way.

Suggested Prayer

Heavenly Father, please renew my vision of you and your plan for my life. Show me especially how you can use me to show your love to my husband.

A Practical Suggestion

If you know other Christians who seem to be genuinely on fire for God, try to find an opportunity to talk with them, and ask them if they can tell you how they keep close to him and in tune with his will.

I do not know how to speak. JEREMIAH 1:6

Read: Jeremiah 1:4-19

Only very rarely was Irene lost for words, but this was one of those occasions. Through a friend at work she had been invited to a women's breakfast meeting run by a local church. It was to take place at a hotel, and a famous sports personality was going to be there to talk about her faith. Irene loved sports, so she agreed to go.

Irene listened intently to the athlete's talk, enthralled by the stories of demanding training in all types of weather, together with her insights into what goes on behind the scenes at competitions. However, Irene found herself even more captivated by the athlete's openness as she talked of her sense of inner need and emptiness, even when competing successfully and winning awards. She told her audience how she became fulfilled only after she turned to Jesus Christ, entrusting her life and future to him. For Irene, who had long had similar feelings herself, this was highly relevant, and when an invitation was given to anyone who wanted to receive Christ, she responded.

As she was driving home it suddenly dawned on Irene that Barry, her husband, did not even know she had gone to a church-run meeting—and he certainly wouldn't expect the news that she'd become a Christian! Turning the corner onto their street, she prayed her first spontaneous prayer, asking God to help her tell Barry. He did, just as he reassured Jeremiah when he felt inadequate. God always helps those who want to tell others about him.

Suggested Prayer
Dear Lord, even though it is hard, please give me the courage to tell people who are close to me, and especially my husband, that you are my Savior and Lord.

A Practical Suggestion
When you feel it is the right time to share your faith with someone, pray for the right words to begin. Then open your mouth, speak them out, and trust God for what follows.

Now you are the people of God. 1 PETER 2:10

Read: 1 Peter 2:4-12

Kara's morale was at an all-time low as she thought about her Christian life. Wanting to see her family and friends become Christians, she had attended an outreach training course at her church, where she learned the key elements of the gospel, different ways to share her testimony, and how to help someone find God's love and forgiveness. The only snag was, it had been two years since the course, and so far Kara had not led anyone to Christ. She was certain she was a second-rate Christian and totally useless to God.

Her main motivation in attending the course had been to help her husband, Norman, believe in Jesus. He was not opposed to the Christian faith and happily attended church on special occasions, but he hadn't yet seen the need to make a decision about Jesus Christ for himself. She had presumed—maybe naively as she saw it now—that if she attended a course and learned the right evangelistic techniques, Norman would soon become her first convert. When he didn't, she began to feel like a failure as a Christian.

One particular Sunday Kara was despondent and tempted not to go to church, but by lunchtime she was glad she did. The sermon that day reminded her of her status and position in Christ. She had been chosen by him; she was one of his privileged people; she belonged to God. Even if her husband had not yet come to Christ, God still loved her deeply. She was not a second-rate Christian at all!

Suggested Prayer
Please remind me often, Lord, how special I am to you. Show me that you love me not for what I do, but because I am just "me."

A Question to Answer
Have you ever sat and meditated for five minutes on how amazing it is that God chose you to be part of his family? Try it!

This poor widow has put in more than all the others. LUKE 21:3

Read: Luke 21:1-4

Beryl tried her hardest to be very discreet about her feelings toward Anna, her friend at church. Actually, Anna was not the problem at all; it was some of the other women who knew them both and made what Beryl considered to be very unfair comparisons. Both Beryl and Anna had husbands at home who were not Christians, and these other women noticed how often Anna's husband accompanied her to church events, while Beryl's husband hardly ever came at all. Beryl always felt that she was perceived as a second-class Christian because her husband was seen at church much less often.

Jesus' comments about the Jewish widow, who, of course, had been parted from her husband altogether, showed that the obvious outward appearance is not always indicative of the true reality of a situation. In this case, the person who gave the least to the temple treasury actually gave most, because it was a far greater proportion of her overall wealth. She probably never knew Jesus was watching her and that he commented to his disciples about her faith, but Jesus wanted his friends to learn an important lesson.

It is so easy for women like Beryl to feel overshadowed by others who appear better, more spiritual, or more successful. In reality, this may or may not be the case. What matters is that Beryl, and others like her, keep in close contact with God, seek to follow him faithfully, and stop worrying about what other people say. God alone knows how complex these situations are!

Suggested Prayer
Help me, Lord, to listen primarily to you. Protect me from hurtful comments from those who neither know my heart and motives, nor my husband's.

A Practical Suggestion
Do not allow yourself to start judging other people if you do not want them to do the same to you.

Like a gold ring in a pig's snout is a beautiful woman who shows no discretion. PROVERBS 11:22

Read: Proverbs 11:16-31

Life at home between Randy and Kristen had rarely been easy since they married. Both were fairly volatile, and it was a source of great relief for everyone when Kristen became a Christian and, almost overnight, began to mellow and become more relaxed. Even this did not prevent some occasional verbal explosions in their home. After these, Kristen increasingly felt the need to unload her feelings onto Christian friends whom she knew would understand and support her.

Jane and Belinda, two established Christians, had grown very close to Kristen since her conversion, and had made it clear that they would always be there to help her when she needed it. After one particularly trying incident at home Kristen went to see them, but Randy followed her to the apartment complex where the young women lived. He started shouting at Kristen before she got inside the building, accusing her of telling her friends confidential information about their relationship that was no business of theirs.

Once the trauma had died down Kristen had time to think about what had happened, and she realized that her husband had a reason to be upset with her. She had no right to betray him by criticizing him to others. God had given her loyal Christian friends whom she appreciated very much, and whom she knew would do anything to support her. But now she also understood that while her friends are available for her anytime—and this is a wonderful privilege—she needs to use discretion about involving them in the intimate problems of her marriage.

Suggested Prayer

Lord, please help me to be careful what I say about my husband to others, even my closest friends. Give me the self-control I need so that I never unintentionally betray him.

A Practical Suggestion

Do not only count to ten before you verbally explode to one of your friends about your husband when he has irritated you; try to find the time and presence of mind to think through what you will say, too.

Pray for those who persecute you. MATTHEW 5:44

Read: Matthew 5:43-48

Eileen knew her situation was unusual. One of her colleagues at work, Jim, was her husband's best friend, and she enjoyed a happy relationship with him as they worked and socialized together. Indeed, there had never been a cross word spoken between them in almost a quarter of a century.

When Eileen became a Christian, however, things began to change. A female colleague at work had become good friends with her, and little by little had told Eileen how much her faith meant to her. The day came when Eileen placed her own trust in Jesus Christ. Jim had taken a dislike to Eileen's friend, and he reported to her husband he thought Eileen was getting indoctrinated. Consequently, when Eileen went home and told her husband about her new faith, he reacted negatively. At work the next morning Jim had a different attitude toward Eileen, even at times making sarcastic comments to and about her. What for so long had been a genuinely happy relationship seemed now to be tainted by his disapproval.

Eileen wasn't sure how to respond. As the words of Jesus' Sermon on the Mount flooded into her mind, she decided not to fight back with sarcasm, nor allow herself to feel hurt or offended so that she became angry. She opted to keep mainly silent. She sensed that Jim had problems understanding God, so if she retaliated it would help no one. She decided to pray hard both for Jim and her husband.

Suggested Prayer

Father, when it is easier for me to lash out with anger because people misunderstand my faith in you, please help me to meditate on how Jesus responded in similar circumstances.

A Practical Suggestion

If you find yourself seething with anger because of some injustice that is either directed at you or someone close to you, quickly find a safe way of releasing it.

Pray for us. COLOSSIANS 4:3

Read: Colossians 4:2-6

Annie was feeling low the day the mailman delivered an airmail letter to her home. That morning she had had a traumatic argument with Bernie, her husband. With some trepidation, she had told him she wanted to go on a special weekend retreat with the women from her church. His reaction was as negative as she feared. He accused her of liking the company of her friends at church much more than his and refused to listen to anything she said in reply. Then he stormed out the door and went to work.

Nursing hurt feelings, Annie sat down to read the letter, telling herself that no one she knew suffered in their marriage as much as she did. The contents of the letter shocked Annie into seeing her own situation in perspective. The letter was from Cynthia, a good friend from church who had moved with her husband and family to Germany a year earlier, when her husband accepted a position with his company as their European liaison. Both Annie and Cynthia had been part of a fellowship group made up largely of Christian women whose husbands did not share their faith. Now Cynthia was writing to say that her husband had quit his job and run off with his German secretary, leaving her and their three young children to fend for themselves in a foreign country. She asked Annie and her friends from church to pray. Annie quickly put aside any thoughts of her own problems and mobilized the prayer support Cynthia had asked for.

Paul sent a letter to the church in Colossae asking the Christians there to pray for him. The apostle knew that physical distance between Christians is no hindrance at all to God. Prayers uttered in one country can affect people radically on the other side of the world. The prayers of Annie and her friends were vital to Cynthia in her time of crisis.

Suggested Prayer

I want to be faithful in praying for others as well as myself, Lord. As I do, help me to have the faith to believe that you can work powerfully.

A Practical Suggestion

Write to or phone someone today who lives out of your own area to encourage them and to find out how you can best pray for them.

Then the fire of the Lord fell. 1 KINGS 18:38

Read: 1 Kings 18:16-39

One morning Katie was desperate for reassurance that God both understood how she felt and still loved her. She knew that during the previous night she had said some terrible things to Joey when he eventually admitted that he was having an affair with someone at work. Not only was this humiliating for Katie but it was also a huge disappointment. She had been praying for her husband to become a Christian ever since making her own commitment to Jesus three years earlier. Now his conversion seemed more unlikely than ever. Katie was not even sure their marriage could survive.

While she knew she could do with some encouragement from friends, Katie felt she couldn't face anyone. She opted to stay at home alone. Joey had gone off to work as usual, the children were at school, and Katie, who had only dozed the night before, slumped into her favorite armchair accompanied by her Bible and a mug of strong coffee. After all the screaming, tears, pain, and name-calling of the night before, she wanted to know whether God was still there for her. If she could feel his presence, she could just about cope with another day.

Many times during the course of human history, God has burst into people's lives and situations at just the right moment. Elijah experienced this, as did the psalmist (see Ps 30:2). Katie's cry was that God would do the same for her. She needed to know his presence, forgiveness, and love, together with some fresh hope and direction for the future.

Suggested Prayer
When I feel at my lowest, Lord, please meet me at my point of deepest need. Give me the reassurance that you will never leave me nor forsake me.

A Practical Suggestion
Read Psalm 30.

Lord, even the demons submit to us in your name. LUKE 10:17

Read: Luke 10:1-20

Ruby was about to burst! Nothing was going to stop her from rushing around to tell her good news to all the members of her fellowship group after church one Sunday. They had specifically prayed for her the previous Wednesday evening when she'd arrived at the meeting rather despondent. Ruby had been a Christian for two years, but felt that her faith had made no noticeable impact on David, her husband. She was desperate for him to become a Christian too.

The group had prayed that Ruby would find a time when she could talk with David and tell him simply and concisely what Jesus had done for her. The right time emerged on Saturday night. With some trepidation lest he ridicule her, she began to speak. Ruby sensed God's gentle presence and was reassured that her friends were praying for her. To her amazement, David listened seriously and responded with both interest and respect. He even said that he had noticed a helpful change in some of her attitudes and, to cap it all, he told her again that he loved her.

Ruby was beside herself with joy on Sunday morning. Just as Jesus had sent out his disciples in mission, she felt that he had called her to tell David about her faith. Now that she had, she too had good news to report. True, David was not a Christian yet, but he seemed closer than ever before!

Suggested Prayer
Father, please give me the courage to tell people what I love about you in a simple and concise way.

A Practical Suggestion
As it can sometimes be easier to talk seriously with your husband if you go out, try to fix a time in the next few days when the two of you can escape for a couple of hours. Then tell him a little about your faith if God gives you the opportunity.

Trusting a Caring God

Not what I will, but what you will. MARK 14:36

Read: Mark 14:32-41

Roseanne had had enough of her stormy seven-year marriage. She and Alex had a volatile relationship, with few periods of calm between the storms. The frequency of their heated arguments and fights had accelerated since she'd become a Christian, mostly because Alex did not like her going to services and meetings at church. He could be loud and abusive when irritated, and while Roseanne had the capacity to respond in a similar way, she now tried hard to honor God by being subdued.

One weekend pushed her over the edge. The tension in the house was extreme, although Roseanne had little idea as to what had caused it. She could only conclude that it was a buildup of unresolved issues. On Sunday afternoon she could no longer tolerate the stress. If marriage provoked such anguish and pain, she would much prefer to be single again.

The next day, as she poured out her heart to a Christian friend, Roseanne had to face a difficult question. Was this what God wanted for her and Alex? her friend asked. Roseanne admitted she had not sought God's will for her marriage but promised to do so now. Roseanne went home and got on her knees, putting the question to God: "Lord, what do you want us to do?" She did not hear God directly, but gradually, over the next few days, she began to realize that getting a divorce would probably be the "easy" way out. The prospect of facing up to their problems, getting help to work through the areas of contention, and then making changes in their attitudes and behavior was not appealing, but deep down she sensed it was probably the better way.

Suggested Prayer

I want to include you in all the major decisions of my life, Lord. Please forgive me when I make independent decisions without asking you first.

A Question to Answer

Can you recall anyone in the Bible whose life became more unbearable in the long-run because they asked for God's guidance and then obeyed it?

Coping with Disappointment

Let us not give up meeting together. HEBREWS 10:25

Read: Hebrews 10:19-25

When they married both Mandy and Craig were committed Christians, but in the years that followed, Craig's relationship with God slowly slipped away. He had gone through a number of family traumas, and had faced some deep disillusionment over problems he'd encountered in the church and with other Christians. Through all this, Mandy tried to stay close to God, but it was not easy.

Craig stopped attending church when the weather turned cold, so while Mandy took the children, he sat happily at home reading the Sunday paper. Once the summer weather arrived, Craig wanted to go out for the day on Sundays and he put pressure on Mandy to join him. This put her in an impossible position. She wanted to remain loyal both to God and her husband, and had no desire to feel guilty in the presence of either of them. Not surprisingly, she sometimes felt angry that because Craig had slipped away from God, she now had to choose between them.

As time went on, Mandy realized she was in danger of losing Craig altogether if she couldn't learn to be flexible and cooperative. Her deep conviction was that one day Craig would come back to the Lord. After talking and praying with her pastor, she told Craig she was willing to skip church every third week to spend some family time together. She hoped dearly that this would be a short-term measure, because she felt uneasy when Sundays passed by and she and the children had not been at church. God's desire for Mandy was her desire too—to meet often with other members of his family.

Suggested Prayer
Lord, when I face circumstances that make me feel I'm in a no-win situation, please give me the insight to make wise decisions.

A Question to Answer

Are you being flexible enough to handle responsibly the many demands on your time, as well as balance your personal need to spend time with God and his family?

He is the image of the invisible God. COLOSSIANS 1:15

Read: Colossians 1:15-23

Having studied theology and world religions at a prestigious university, John was not going to allow anyone, including his wife, to suggest that he was unfamiliar with the Bible. However, that was how it came across after Tracy returned home from a church retreat weekend. She had only gone because a friend had invited her, saying it would be fun, but now Tracy seemed passionate about Jesus Christ in a way that John found very hard to grasp.

Being the son of a university religion professor, John had always found theology intriguing, even at a very young age. He had followed in his father's footsteps and pursued both undergraduate and graduate degrees in religion. He studied and evaluated all kinds of religions, but was never tempted to view them as anything more than fodder for academic study and research. Indeed, John could not understand those "fanatics" who attended church and spoke of God and Jesus Christ in emotive terms. Privately, he despised them and felt they were wildly misguided. He was not concerned whether there was a true God or not, and whether Jesus Christ did or did not exist.

However, John found himself having to confront these issues now that Tracy had come home claiming to have a personal relationship with God. He could not dispute that she seemed genuinely happy, and, though excited about her new faith, she seemed controlled, not fanatical. Faced with the evidence of a transformed wife, John began to read the Bible again. Could it really be true that Almighty God existed, and that Jesus Christ came to earth to make him known?

Suggested Prayer
Please let my life be a strong witness for you wherever I go, Lord, especially at home. Help others to see Jesus living in me.

A Practical Suggestion

Reflect honestly about your life, and think about any of your actions or attitudes that probably make it harder for other people to believe in Jesus. Repent when you are ready, and ask God to help you change.

God our Savior ... wants all men to be saved. 1 TIMOTHY 2:3-4

Read: 1 Timothy 2:1-7

Recent research gleaned from Christian wives reveals that just nine percent of their unbelieving husbands go to church with them. Bert is one who does, although he would argue that he is a Christian too. He insists that since he grew up in a Christian family in a Christian country and lives by the Ten Commandments, he has the right to call himself a Christian. Emily, his wife, has tried to explain to him many times that being a Christian is more than this, but it has made no difference.

Sparks flew one Sunday when Bert, certain he was expressing a "Christian" point of view, argued with Tim, the minister, outside church after the service. Tim had preached with conviction about the dire needs of refugees in parts of Africa and had asked the church to take an extra offering for them. Bert disputed that this was a priority, and insisted that "we shouldn't worry about Africans until we've taken care of homeless people in our own country."

Back home Bert gave Emily a hard time when she openly sided with Tim. The next day over coffee in Tim's study, Emily explained her view of Bert's misunderstanding of Christianity. Tim agreed to visit Bert to continue their discussion, but encouraged Emily to get some close friends together for prayer. "There is no doubt that God loves Bert deeply, but we need to pray that Bert will be open enough to rethink the distorted Christianity with which he has grown up," Tim said.

Suggested Prayer
Lord, because you love my husband even more than I do and want him to be part of your family, please answer my heartfelt prayers for him.

A Practical Suggestion
If your husband is happy to attend church with you, ask him to join you at a special seminar or course that includes a clear presentation of the gospel.

David found strength in the Lord his God. 1 SAMUEL 30:6

Read: 1 Samuel 30:1-20

Although she certainly was not looking for trouble, Betty found that she and Jack were often at loggerheads. They had been married for over thirty years, and their children had grown up and left home. They'd gotten along pretty well for most of their marriage, but Jack had grown sullen and hard to live with ever since Betty's conversion to Christianity five years ago. Jack had always considered religion a colossal waste of time, and he was appalled the day Betty told him she'd committed her life to God.

Different things aggravated Jack at different times. Whenever he found Betty reading the Bible, he always snapped, "Why don't you go to the library and get a decent book to read?" He grumbled about her going to church on Sunday mornings, but not too loudly, since it gave him a couple of hours of "peace and quiet" to putz around in the backyard and tend to his prize begonias. He seemed most annoyed at the church meetings that took her out in the evenings—time they had always enjoyed together relaxing in front of the TV or playing card games. When she got home after an evening meeting, she always found him moody and uncommunicative.

Through no fault of his own David found himself unpopular with his men. This was when he looked to God for strength, and was filled again with divine resources. The good news is that in her difficult situation, Betty can do the same.

Suggested Prayer

Heavenly Father, please give me the sensitivity I need to make wise decisions at home, and strengthen me as I trust in you today. Thank you that your resources will be sufficient whatever I have to face.

A Practical Suggestion

Find time today to take a walk so that you can think and pray. As you do, ask God to show you again how rich and powerful his resources are.

Be patient, then, brothers. JAMES 5:7

Read: James 5:7-11

James wrote his New Testament letter to readers who seemed impatient that Jesus had not yet returned as he promised. Little did they know that two thousand years later Christians would still be waiting! James encouraged his readers to get on with serving the Lord and standing firm for him, not worrying about when he would return. Becoming impatient that God has not yet worked as we expected is futile.

Glenda is a young Christian woman who is still waiting for the fulfillment of God's promises. She is a modern-day Christian to whom James' admonishment to keep praying is just as needed as it was in the first century. Glenda married Darren two years after another couple, who had also met in the local church's youth group, held their wedding. At that time, the wife in the other relationship was a Christian, although her husband was not. However, within eighteen months he too had become a dedicated follower of Jesus Christ. This encouraged Glenda, because when she and Darren married he showed only scant interest in her faith. She anticipated that if she prayed a lot and witnessed to him at home, he would soon commit his life to God.

Two years later Darren was no closer to responding, and Glenda was becoming disillusioned. She felt he would never be saved, and at this stage, of course, no one could be sure. Christian salvation depends not only on God's Holy Spirit working in a person's life, but also on an individual's positive response to the grace of God.

The best thing Glenda can do is to take James' words to heart, and to keep praying and being a strong witness. God will fulfill all his promises in time, but we must keep serving him while we wait.

Suggested Prayer

Please help me to keep my eyes on you and your strength, Lord, when I might otherwise be tempted to focus on what has not yet happened.

A Practical Suggestion

Read one of the psalms that contains exhilarating praise and worship addressed to God.

Not Jumping to Conclusions

Do not judge, or you too will be judged. MATTHEW 7:1

Read: Matthew 7:1-6

Alison was not sure whether to bite her lip or explode. She was listening to a discussion in her adult Sunday school class that brought back painful memories of events with which she had not yet fully come to terms. Before she moved and settled into this church, she had been part of a fellowship where she felt tried and condemned in her absence. She had missed church for a couple of weeks due to family reunions, and other factors had forced her to be away from three fellowship meetings in succession. The next she heard was that some church members had concluded that her commitment, both to God and the church, must be extremely shallow if she attended as irregularly as she did. Angry and hurt at the way she'd been judged, Alison was relieved when her husband's job forced them to move a hundred miles north. God was important to her, but, with her husband not being a Christian, she found life was often extremely complicated.

She had joined the adult Sunday school class in her new church, expecting that things would be different here. Needless to say, Alison was extremely disturbed that Sunday morning to hear them discussing who was missing from the class and why. When mention was made of another young woman who was married to an unbeliever, someone commented on her apparent lack of dedication. Alison erupted inside and was faced with the dilemma of whether or not to tell the story of her own pain and hurt. Should she speak out or keep quiet?

Suggested Prayer
Please help me not to judge others, Lord, especially those whose circumstances are virtually unknown to me. Let your love flow from me as it did from Jesus.

A Question to Answer
Have you repented before God, and maybe apologized to the person involved, for the last time you were judgmental of someone?

The God of all grace ... will ... make you strong, firm and steadfast.
1 PETER 5:10

Read: 1 Peter 5:1-11

At times, Lindy wondered if it was all worth it. To run away from everyone and everything seemed an appealing possibility. Life at home was tough. Ray, her husband, had been out of work for four years and increasingly lacked the motivation to pursue any jobs he saw advertised. Most days he sat in his armchair in front of the television expecting Lindy to get him food and drink when she wasn't at work herself. He resented it whenever she went out, particularly to church and to meet her Christian friends. He believed she should be there with him as often as possible.

As if this were not enough, Lindy also had other things to contend with. Ray's unemployment meant that they barely had enough money on which to live, and the children were having to do without a lot of necessities their friends all took for granted. Lindy felt bad about this, as she did about the single man at church whom she often caught looking at her. That she found him attractive too simply compounded her sense of guilt. It is no wonder that Lindy felt trapped, frustrated, and unhappy.

Lindy has only to confess her weakness and vulnerability to God and he will come to her and give her new strength. The apostle Peter knew from personal experience how easy it is to succumb to temptation when we take our eyes off Jesus. But if we keep our focus firmly on him, he is able to provide new spiritual strength to carry on in the face of enormous pressure. Furthermore, he can help us resist the devil's subtle and appealing temptations.

Suggested Prayer

Father, please help me to entrust any anxiety and pain I have to you. Thank you that whatever is going on in my life, you love me and want to strengthen me so that I can live for you.

A Practical Suggestion

Ask your friends to suggest the name of other Christians who have had to cope with serious problems, but come through their difficulties stronger with God's help. Try to arrange to talk with one of those people to gain encouragement.

Taking a Long Time

One who was there had been an invalid for thirty-eight years. JOHN 5:5

Read: John 5:1-15

Elsie could not believe how long it had been. She was just a couple of years from retirement and had been a Christian for over thirty years, having been converted soon after she and Ted married. For all this time she had prayed for Ted to become a Christian too, but so far it had not happened. At times she became disillusioned, but on the whole she remained philosophical and kept using special opportunities to invite Ted to church events which would expose him yet again to the gospel.

Ted didn't mind this. He knew and understood Christianity sufficiently to know that he was still on the outside. Occasionally he heard personal testimonies in church when people told how their lives had been changed by Jesus Christ, often dramatically. Ted respected what he heard, but at no point did he feel compelled to make any decision for himself. He was not unhappy as he was, although he recognized that some of the Christians he met seemed to have a greater sense of purpose in their lives than he did. Meanwhile, Elsie kept praying.

The man Jesus met at the pool called Bethesda had been unable to walk for thirty-eight years. However, like Elsie, he still hoped that something miraculous would happen one day. His dreams were realized when he met Jesus. Often you have to wait a long time, but then, seemingly out of the blue, Jesus does something dramatic. Elsie must keep on praying.

Suggested Prayer
Lord, please encourage me when I find it hard to cope because my prayers have not yet been answered. Help me to keep trusting you however long it takes.

A Question to Answer
Do you realize that God often seems to wait before answering our prayers in order to find out how serious we are about what we are asking him?

— Also Available —

Unbelieving Husbands
and the Wives Who Love Them
Michael Fanstone

Thousands of hurting women agonize over a common, painful heartache: Their husbands, the men they love most in the world, do not love the Lord. Michael J. Fanstone, a seasoned pastor and author, has counseled scores of women burdened by this sad and frustrating situation.

Without making promises that it can't keep, *Unbelieving Husbands and the Wives Who Love Them* offers sound advice and warm encouragement for wives who want the very best for the man they married. $10.99

Available from your local Christian bookstore
or from Servant Publications, P.O. Box 8617,
Ann Arbor, Michigan 48107.

Please include payment plus $3.25 shipping and handling for
each copy ordered.